THE FOUR
LEADER
OF JESUS

THE FOURFOLD
LEADERSHIP
OF JESUS

Come, follow, wait, go

ANDREW WATSON

Text copyright © Andrew Watson 2008
The author asserts the moral right
to be identified as the author of this work

Published by
The Bible Reading Fellowship
15 The Chambers, Vineyard
Abingdon OX14 3FE
Website: www.brf.org.uk

ISBN 978 1 84101 435 7
First published 2008
10 9 8 7 6 5 4 3 2 1 0
All rights reserved

Acknowledgments
Unless otherwise stated, scripture quotations are taken from the Holy Bible,
Today's New International Version, copyright © 2004 by International Bible
Society, are used by permission of Hodder & Stoughton Publishers, a division of
Hodder Headline Ltd. All rights reserved. 'TNIV' is a registered trademark of
International Bible Society.

Scripture quotations from the Holy Bible, New International Version, copyright ©
1973, 1978, 1984 by International Bible Society, are used by permission of
Hodder & Stoughton Publishers, a division of Hodder Headline Ltd. All rights
reserved. 'NIV' is a registered trademark of International Bible Society. UK
trademark number 1448790.

The Holy Bible, English Standard Version, copyright © 2001 by Crossway Bibles,
a division of Good News Publishers.

New English Bible copyright © 1961, 1970 by Oxford University Press and
Cambridge University Press.

Scripture quotations from The Revised Standard Version of the Bible, copyright ©
1946, 1952, 1971 by the Division of Christian Education of the National Council
of the Churches of Christ in the United States of America, are used by permission.
All rights reserved.

Extracts from the Authorized Version of the Bible (The King James Bible), the
rights in which are vested in the Crown, are reproduced by permission of the
Crown's patentee, Cambridge University Press.

Extracts from the Book of Common Prayer of 1662, the rights of which are vested
in the Crown in perpetuity within the United Kingdom, are reproduced by
permission of Cambridge University Press, Her Majesty's Printers.

A catalogue record for this book is available from the British Library

Printed in Singapore by Craft Print International Ltd

CONTENTS

Foreword 6

Introduction: Come, follow, wait, go 7

Part 1: 'Come to me'

1   Accessible leadership...22

2   The character of the shepherd 29

3   Jesus' access to the Father...41

4   Living within easy reach 46

Part 2: 'Follow me'

5   Inspirational leadership 58

6   The character of the pioneer and perfecter........................69

7   Jesus' obedience to the Father..80

8   Walking the way of costly grace 86

Part 3: 'Wait for me'

9   Long-term leadership...98

10 The character of the farmer 107

11 Jesus' trust in the Father 116

12 Embracing the call to passionate patience 124

Part 4: 'Go for me'

13 Multiplying leadership...136

14 The character of our Lord 145

15 Jesus' calling from the Father...154

16 Responding to the missionary challenge 161

Conclusion: Leaders, followers and the character of Jesus 171

Notes 179

✤

FOREWORD

The most critical question facing the Church in the West today concerns discipleship. How can we live authentic and consistent Christian lives in a globalized consumer world? The evangelizing of Western culture does not depend on 'fresh expressions of church' alone. It depends on the quality of the disciples that both fresh expressions and more traditional churches make. It is this challenge that makes leadership such an important matter. Without appropriate leadership, we will never get appropriate discipleship.

That is what makes Andrew Watson's book so pertinent. He understands that Jesus was a disciple, making disciples, who commissioned his followers to keep on making disciples. All talk of Jesus as a leader needs to be understood in that context. In various books, Dallas Willard has reminded us that taking Jesus seriously requires us to accept that Jesus knows how to live our lives better than we do. This book applies that to Jesus as a leader. Andrew is a very experienced leader and teacher who realizes that Jesus knows how to lead even better than he does, and who is determined to continue to be a disciple as well as a leader.

Andrew draws illustrations from his own experience, but this book is more than a compilation of helpful insights. It is the result of a journey from life to scripture and back again. Real leadership teaches wise leaders what they most need to learn. It is his experience as a leader that raised this question in Andrew's mind and took him back to Jesus, to learn from the great disciple-making leader. As a result, fresh insights have been identified and made available for us all in this very helpful book.

+ *Graham Maidstone*

✣

COME, FOLLOW, WAIT, GO

'Don't follow me. Follow Jesus!'

It was a sticker attached to the rear window of the car in front; and as I sat in an interminable London traffic jam, I had plenty of time for the message to sink in.

At first sight it seemed humble, gracious, eminently reasonable. 'I'm a Christian,' the driver in front was proclaiming, 'but not much of a Christian, I'm afraid. I'm all too aware of my faults and failings. Perhaps you'll be aware of them, too, as driving isn't always my strong point. Jesus—now he's the perfect driver. Follow him and you won't go wrong. That's all I wanted to say, actually. Thanks for listening.' A gentle, straightforward piece of Christian witnessing, it seemed, and certainly somewhat clearer to the average secularist than the ubiquitous *icthus* fish.

Yet as I reflected further, the message of the sticker began to trouble me. It was partly that it seemed to assume a culture in which 'following Jesus' was common currency, a society well-versed in the Gospels and adept at making links between Jesus' day and our own; and such a view of 21st-century London appeared naïve in the extreme.[1] But it was also that the message seemed dangerously convenient, a neat get-out clause for every Christian believer who wished to avoid the challenge of personal holiness and to hide behind the one they were called upon to follow.

The apostle Paul, I pondered, had no such qualms. 'Follow my example, as I follow the example of Christ' was his call to the church in Corinth (1 Corinthians 11:1), and similar commands are liberally scattered throughout his letters.[2] Here, by contrast, was a man who acknowledged the need to live out the life of Jesus in his generation:

not just pointing his readers to a book, or teaching them a series of lifestyle principles, but recognizing that his first calling as a Christian leader was to embody the message of his crucified, risen Lord.

And while the sentiment of the car sticker might be superficially attractive, the challenge of Paul's position was undeniable, and his logic was compelling. A sad reality is that most people today will never read a Gospel, runs the logic. Its sobering counterpart is that those selfsame people will frequently 'read' the Christians who are called to embody it.

The sticker in the window of the car in front, and the call to 'follow my example, as I follow the example of Christ', first planted in me the idea of writing this book. For one thing, Paul's words suggested a way of life to which every Christian believer should aspire: being the 'salt of the earth', the 'light of the world' and 'yeast in the dough', in Jesus' famous metaphors (Matthew 5:13–16; Luke 13:20–21). For another, they contained a striking, even revelatory insight—that leadership and discipleship are so closely related as to be virtually indistinguishable from one another.

The context of 1 Corinthians 11:1 makes this point still clearer. Here was Paul writing to a church that combined great spiritual fervour with alarming spiritual immaturity. Among their more childish characteristics was a tendency to division based on personality cults: 'I follow Paul,' said one; 'I follow Apollos,' another; 'I follow Cephas,' a third; to which the fourth would respond—perhaps somewhat smugly—'I follow Christ!' (1 Corinthians 1:12). In such a context it would have been easy for Paul to support the 'I follow Christ' brigade. Clever children, after all, quickly discover that 'Jesus' is generally the right answer to any question posed by their Sunday school teacher. The fact that Paul formulated it quite so differently seemed highly significant against such a backdrop. To the Corinthians, after all, Jesus was invisible. It was now up to the second generation of Christian disciples, Paul himself and the 'body of Christ' in Corinth, to live out the life of Jesus lovingly, faithfully and with gospel integrity.

Up to that point, I had read, listened and taught much on leadership. I read books that focused on learnt techniques and practices—casting a vision, developing a strategy, building a team, dealing with conflict—and I read books that were far more centred on personality and self-understanding. I learnt my Myers Briggs profile,[3] completed my Belbin inventory[4] and knew my five top strengths in the Strengthsfinder exercise.[5] The best of such approaches had proved hugely positive and illuminating and helped to develop my self-understanding and shape my leadership practices.

Yet at times I had become uneasy and frustrated at much of the leadership material on offer—or, at least, increasingly aware of its limitations. There seemed to be a frequent attempt to 'baptize' secular management theories: to see Jesus as the ultimate CEO, someone at ease at the head of the table in a major multinational corporation, moving it from 'good' to 'great' with consummate skill. There seemed to be a regular shift in language and meaning—the word 'vision', for example, moving from a powerful, God-given encounter to a long (and frequently tedious) process of consultation followed by the eventual drawing-up of a five-year strategic plan. There seemed to be a danger that personality tools would move from the realm of description to prescription, thus closing the door on a God for whom 'all things are possible' (Mark 10:27) and whose 'power is made perfect in weakness' (2 Corinthians 12:9). Yes, there were lessons to be learnt, but sometimes those lessons appeared tangential to the heart of Christian leadership.

Another debate consumed both time and energy, polarizing Christians between those who stressed 'doing' and those in favour of simply 'being'. Some leadership books I read left me exhausted with the sheer activism of their writers—generally highly successful church leaders who had grown a church from 300 to 3000 in a matter of months. Their motto was 'It's better to burn out than rust out', and their role model was Paul at the height of his missionary endeavours, moving from city to city with alarming rapidity and extraordinary effectiveness. Other books, usually written by those of a more Catholic persuasion, were far more contemplative in tone. Their motto was 'We are called to be human beings, not human doings', and their champion was Mary of Bethany, who had chosen 'what is better' by sitting at the feet of Jesus—so earning his commendation in contrast to her workaholic and bad-tempered sister (Luke 10:38–42).

I read books on episcopal ministry, on priestly ministry, on lay ministry and on ministry teams. I read books on women's ministry and a book somewhat directly entitled *Leadership is Male*.[6] I read an alarming book which suggested that leaders under 45 were far more likely to lead growing churches than those over 45[7]—alarming in that I had just celebrated my 45th birthday. And meanwhile, I was teaching at a number of leadership conferences in Norway, Sweden and the UK, sharing some of the insights I was picking up along the way, but also wanting to wrestle with the Christian scriptures—allowing them to speak with an authentic voice rather than squeezing them into the box of 21st-century management theory.

That sticker in the car window, and its antithesis in 1 Corinthians 11, therefore opened up for me a new way of looking at things, an approach where Christian character—nothing less than the imitation of Christ—was thrust into the forefront of the leadership debate.

If discipleship and leadership are quite so closely related, then— if our authority to lead is directly proportionate to the quality of our discipleship—Christians can enter that debate with a unique and distinctive voice. Indeed, theirs will be a vital contribution at a time when traditional authority structures are increasingly derided, when issues of integrity are at the forefront of the political and commercial agendas, and when only those leaders who practise what they preach—Nelson Mandela, Mother Teresa, Martin Luther King, to name but three—are regarded as both credible and safe to follow.

At first sight, this approach seems to side with the 'being' brigade. We need to be like Jesus, and how do we do that? Presumably through the traditional disciplines of prayer and fasting, solitude and silence—taking our place on the floor beside Mary of Bethany. Yet Jesus was a man of action as much as a man of prayer. Following him must therefore involve doing as much as being, the two neatly encapsulated in Mark 3:14–15: '[Jesus] appointed twelve—designating them apostles—that they might be with him and that he might send them out to preach and to have authority to drive out demons.'

Imitating Christ cannot dispense with the need for spiritual discipline (being with Jesus), but neither can it ignore the challenge of kingdom activity, the call to 'preach and… drive out demons'. The growth towards a Christ-like character includes the extravert challenge of mission alongside the introvert challenge of a deeper communion with the Father. Activists need to develop their contemplative side, and contemplatives their missionary activity. Only then are such leaders safe to follow, as those who themselves are seeking, however falteringly, to follow the example of Christ.

JESUS AND LEADERSHIP

The idea that character is key in the life of a leader is hardly a startling one. It is there in the New Testament, most notably in the instructions about overseers and deacons in 1 Timothy 3 and about elders in Titus 1. It is there in the best of the books about Christian leadership, and—in a world where trust is of the essence—it is there in the syllabus of many a business school, theological college and medical training institute.

James Lawrence's *Growing Leaders*[8] helpfully identifies 'calling, character and competence' as the key areas of leadership development, quoting Bill Hybels' definition of character as 'who you are when no one else is looking'. Leighton Ford's *Transforming Leadership*[9] speaks of the empowering nature of Jesus' leadership style and his ability to change situations rather than merely working within them. The description of Jesus as a 'courteous rebel' (itself a quotation from Stephen Neill) particularly stands out for me, as does Ford's own portrayal of the balance of Jesus' character—his apparently contradictory personality traits held in powerful but creative tension. John Adair's *The Leadership of Jesus*[10] compares Jesus' leadership style with that of other leaders of his day and identifies humility as the most distinctive and significant theme in Jesus' life and legacy.

One thing that many writers seem to miss, though, is a startling fact—that Jesus himself virtually never talked about leadership. The Twelve he called to himself would today be called a 'leadership team'. Jesus taught them, he equipped them, and he promised them a key role in the future when they would 'sit on twelve thrones, judging the twelve tribes of Israel' (Matthew 19:28). When one of the team betrayed Jesus and promptly hung himself, Peter made an exegetically adventurous leap from Psalm 109 in his conviction that another should 'take his place of leadership' (Acts 1:20), and Matthias was quickly appointed in Judas' place. Yet throughout the Gospels, Jesus studiously avoided the 'L' word altogether, alongside the other obvious designations of pastors, elders, overseers or priests. His followers were called 'disciples' (literally 'learners') or 'apostles' ('those who are sent'). They were variously described as workers, students, servants, slaves, fishers of people, lambs among wolves and, in a particularly moving passage in John 15, friends. Peter, James and John appeared to form something of an inner core, but James and John's attempts to secure the leadership privileges they might expect from that position were met with a gentle but firm rebuttal (Matthew 20:23).

Peter, it's true, seemed to be uniquely set apart, although the phrase used in Matthew 16:18, 'On this rock I will build my church', was hardly the language of a conventional leadership role. As to why Peter was selected as the first among equals, there are varying opinions, but one obvious attribute singles him out from the rest. Peter was not only the first to acknowledge the true identity of Jesus. It was also Peter who stepped out of the boat and came to Jesus across the water (Matthew 14:28–29), Peter who followed Jesus as far as the courtyard of the high priest (26:58), and Peter who was the first of the apostles to enter the empty tomb (Luke 24:12). He was also there (by invitation) on further significant occasions, from the mount of transfiguration to the garden of Gethsemane.

Not all of these incidents showed the apostle at his best, of course, or would form obvious contenders in a compilation of 'Peter's greatest hits'. But they do demonstrate how this man acted as Jesus' closest follower in a literal sense—following him on to the water, up to the mountain, into the garden, up to the courtroom, into the tomb. Once again the point is made that in Jesus' understanding, leadership and discipleship (or 'followership', to coin a term) amount to very much the same thing.

Jesus' teaching in Matthew 23 is particularly instructive. In the context of a strong critique of the blindness and hypocrisy of the Pharisees, he issued his followers with the clearest of instructions: 'You are not to be called "Rabbi", for you have only one Master and you are all brothers. And do not call anyone on earth "father", for you have one Father, and he is in heaven. Nor are you to be called "teacher", for you have one Teacher, the Messiah. The greatest among you will be your servant' (vv. 8–11). The theme of the greatest being the servant is common to all four Gospels. In Mark it was associated with Jesus' own calling not 'to be served, but to serve, and to give his life as a ransom for many' (10:45). In John it was famously enacted in the visual parable of the foot washing on the night before he died (13:3–4).

These passages more than hint at the reasons behind Jesus' suspicion of 'leadership' as a category in which to place his disciples. First and foremost, his concern sprang out of an understanding of his own mission in terms of service—of giving his life 'as a ransom for many'—and, as he pointed out on several occasions, 'Students are not above their teacher, nor servants above their master' (Matthew 10:24). In other words, if the teacher or master serves, his students or servants would clearly be called to do the same.

In a secondary sense, though, Jesus' own experience told him of the corrupting influence of power on fallen human nature. 'Everything they do is done for people to see,' he said of the Pharisees as he castigated their hypocrisy and self-absorption (Matthew 23:5). 'Do not do what they do' (v. 3). 'You know that those who are regarded as rulers of the Gentiles lord it over them, and their high officials exercise authority over them,' said Jesus of the Roman authorities of his day. 'Not so with you' (Mark 10:42–43).

Underlying such thinking was a long biblical tradition going back to the prophet Samuel and the Israelites' ever more pressing insistence for a king. In those distant days, the prophet had grimly spelt out the implications of the people's demand: 'He will take your sons and make them serve with his chariots and horses… He will take your daughters to be perfumers and cooks and bakers. He will take the best of your fields and vineyards and olive groves… He will take a tenth of your grain… a tenth of your flocks, and you yourselves will become his slaves' (1 Samuel 8:11–17). 'Take, take, take' was the language of kingship in Samuel's understanding, and in that of the prophets who all too frequently witnessed the fulfilment of his stark warning.

It's no wonder that the old categories of power and privilege no longer seemed to fit as the disciples began to follow Christ, and that the old language of 'taking' could only apply in a radically new sense. 'Take my yoke upon you and learn from me… For my yoke is easy and my burden is light' (Matthew 11:29–30).

To say that Jesus was lukewarm on the subject of leadership is therefore something of an understatement. He never gave his followers any designation that smacked of leadership in its normal sense, or took them aside for specifically leadership training. He never passed on his insights into vision-seeking, team-building or time management. It's true that we can extrapolate certain principles from Jesus' own practice in these areas, but the Master's sole concern was to disciple his followers through the word, both spoken and enacted.

From Jesus they learned about the kingdom of God, about humility and prayer, money and generosity, love and purity. From him they learned about forgiveness and grace, healing and proclamation, heaven and hell. They were taught to go and make disciples (Matthew 28:19), to let their light so shine before others 'that they may see your good deeds and glorify your Father in heaven' (5:16). Their leadership calling was simply to say with Paul, 'Follow my example, as I follow the example of Christ', using words if necessary. It was as straightforward, and as supremely challenging, as that.

JESUS THE DISCIPLE

At first sight there is one exception to Jesus' reticence in the Gospel records, and that lies in the description of his own role as leader. In the Gospel accounts, he is variously designated 'Son of Man', 'Son of David', and 'Son of the Living God'. He is additionally described as Teacher, Rabbi, Master and Shepherd. 'You call me "Teacher" and "Lord"', he said at the conclusion of the foot-washing episode, 'and rightly so, for that is what I am' (John 13:13), while seven chapters later, Thomas was responding to his encounter with the risen Christ in the most radical statement of them all: 'My Lord and my God!' (20:28).

If Jesus is indisputably the master, though, there is another strand in the Gospels that portrays him in the role of disciple. In Matthew 12:18 he is explicitly identified with Isaiah's suffering servant, 'the one I love, in whom I delight'—the beginnings of a rich seam of thinking that leads to some of the most powerful insights in all of Christian theology. In Mark 1:12–13, and elsewhere in the Gospels, there is the clear sense of Jesus as a man under authority: 'At once the Spirit sent him out into the wilderness, and he was in the wilderness for forty days, being tempted by Satan.' Prayer was central to Jesus' ministry, communing with a Father who affirmed him, equipped him, directed him and provided for him. The many references to Jesus as a man 'sent' by God imply that Jesus himself was an apostle ('one who is sent'), while the anonymous writer of the letter to the Hebrews placed him in the role of disciple ('learner') when he boldly wrote that Jesus 'learned obedience from what he suffered' (5:8).

It is in John's Gospel that this theme is most fully developed. Jesus 'can do nothing by himself; he can do only what he sees his Father doing, because whatever the Father does the Son also does' (John 5:19). 'What I have heard from him I tell the world', Jesus affirms a few chapters later, and 'I always do what pleases him' (8:26, 29). 'I did not speak on my own', he continues in chapter 12, 'but the Father who sent me commanded me to say all that I have spoken' (v. 49), and the close identification between Jesus and 'the one who sent me' emphasizes both his unique authority and his trusting submission to the will of the Father.

Even Jesus, then, was a disciple called to make disciples. The authority of his leadership was dependent on the quality of his discipleship. In this grand game of 'Follow my leader', rich with cosmic significance, Jesus may be visibly at the front of the queue in the Gospel narratives, but before him is an invisible presence who leads and directs his every step. And it is as the perfect disciple to his heavenly Father—as one whose obedience was tested through the most extreme of human sufferings and triumphantly passed the test—that Jesus' own leadership becomes inspirational, life-giving and supremely fruitful.

'We are only able to imitate and follow a man whom we have before our eyes,' wrote Augustine of Hippo, 'and yet it was necessary for us to follow God who is invisible, and not a mere man. In order then to give us an example we could safely follow, God became a man.'[11]

THE CALL TO DISCIPLESHIP

A brief survey of leadership in the Gospels leads to a clear conclusion: that Jesus' passion was for discipleship rather than leadership; indeed, that, in Jesus' understanding, the two categories entirely overlap.

It's not that leadership competence is unimportant, of course. Nor is it that every true disciple is called to the same leadership role, or chaos would ensue. But character, discipleship, the imitation of Christ, occupies such a pivotal place in the Gospel narratives that every other leadership attribute and charisma (in its secular sense) must constantly be judged in its light. 'Now then these three remain,' we might conclude: 'charisma, competence and character. But the greatest of these is character.'

Set against such a background, the call of Jesus to 'follow me' is not simply a divine call: 'Follow me because I am the Son of God.' It is also a human call: 'Follow me because I myself am the perfect follower.' Neither of those phrases, of course, is true of Paul's leadership, or your leadership or mine. It would be quite inappropriate for any Christian leader to issue a 'Follow me' call without any further qualification. 'At that time if anyone says to you, "Look, here is the Messiah!" ... do not believe it!' (Mark 13:21) would be Jesus' rejoinder to such a foolhardy and, in its original sense, 'misleading' practice. But complete with the qualifying phrase, 'as I follow the example of Christ', the Christian leader's call to 'follow me' is not only acceptable but essential; hence the exhaustive and sometimes exhausting nature of the training of the Twelve, as Jesus worked night and day to form a discipleship group who were, quite simply, safe to follow.

COME, FOLLOW, WAIT, GO

'Follow me', though, was not the only call issued by Jesus to his disciples. There were times when he called people to 'come to me', times when he invited them to 'wait for me', and times when he asked them to 'go for me'. Come, follow, wait, go: each represents a different aspect of the call to discipleship, and each reveals unique facets of the character of Jesus the caller.

The call 'Come to me' suggests a leader who is facing his or her people, arms perhaps outstretched in a gesture of friendliness and warmth. Acceptance and accessibility are the key themes of such an approach, as the leader consciously seeks to reduce the distance between themselves and those they lead. 'Come to me' leadership is therefore strongly relational. At its heart lies an intimate and face-to-face encounter, a meeting that is comforting, enriching and, at times, mutually exposing.

The call 'Follow me', by contrast, implies a leader who is walking ahead of his or her people, with only their back (not their face) on view to those responding to the challenge. Here is a more rugged calling—arguably a more demanding one—as the leader strides ahead, blazing a frequently courageous and uncomfortable trail. The ability to inspire is foundational to the 'Follow me' leader, but it is an inspiration based on actions, not just words. On its own, 'Follow me' may lack compassion and patience, creating a culture of the survival of the fittest, where the casualties are plentiful and the carers are few. But forgo 'Follow me' and organizational drift sets in —a loss of vision, a lack of direction, where the led become increasingly enfeebled and inward-looking, and very little gets done.

Disciples called to 'wait for me' are by definition on their own but are held in that place by a sense of expectation, trust or simple need. 'Wait for me' leadership at its best is faithful, prayerful and patient, and encourages the same qualities in those who are led. It has a wider and longer-term view of God's purposes and how they will come to fruition. Its timing is based on the seasonal world of farming more than the relentless world of industry. And how does it distinguish itself from the laziness and indecision of 'Wait for me' counterfeits? Simply through the sheer quantity and quality of its fruitfulness.

'Go for me' presents the image of a disciple looking out toward the horizon and the leader standing beside them, one hand on their shoulder and the other pointing out the direction in which the disciple needs to go. It may suggest the need to sort something out, perhaps a domestic situation or an area of immaturity or compromise. Yet at heart it forms the substance of a missionary calling, inviting people to step away from their home-based comforts and securities and set out on a journey which is, by its nature, both exciting and scarily unpredictable.

'Come, follow, wait, go': in part they represent different styles of leadership, so most people reading the last four paragraphs will be able (with a little reflection) to recognize those in which they are instinctively strong and those where they struggle. But if Christ himself is our model, the challenge is to embrace all four of these approaches rather than opting for the one or two that are most congenial to our character or temperament. Given the argument of this chapter as a whole, that will involve, first and foremost, a wholehearted commitment not so much to leadership training but to Christian discipleship—coming to Jesus, following him, waiting for his timing and responding to his missionary call.

How, then, do the challenges to come, follow, wait and go shed light on the character of Jesus? And how can we ourselves grow as disciple-leaders, rejecting the feebleness of 'Don't follow me, follow Jesus' and embracing the challenge of 'Follow my example, as I follow the example of Christ'? These are the two questions at the heart of the study on which we now embark.

—— Part 1 ——

COME TO ME

*'Come to me, all you who are weary and
burdened, and I will give you rest.'*

MATTHEW 11:28

✤

─────── 1 ───────

ACCESSIBLE LEADERSHIP

One of the historical oddities referred to in E.H. Gombrich's magnificent book *The Story of Art* is the number of aesthetic movements that were first 'christened' by the critics who derided them.[1] The word 'Gothic', for example, was initially used by Italian art critics to denote a style that they considered barbarous, brought into Italy by the Goths who had effectively destroyed the Roman empire and true culture with it. 'Baroque' means 'grotesque', and was employed by those who insisted on the absurdity of mixing classical forms in ways that went far beyond the good taste of Ancient Greece and Rome. 'Mannerism' and 'Impressionism' were also terms coined by their opponents, and although the first exhibition held by the Impressionists was widely ridiculed ('They take a piece of canvas, colour and brush, and daub a few patches of paint at random, and sign the whole thing with their name,' as one critic put it), it wasn't long before Monet and his friends were wearing the Impressionist badge with pride.

The same may be said of the expression 'Friend of tax collectors and sinners'—a term of abuse used by Jesus' opponents but one that Jesus himself never tried to repudiate. His reputation as a man apparently indifferent to the company he kept—indeed as one who actively sought out the more disreputable members of the society around him—provided constant fuel for a growing swell of gossip and censure instigated by the religious leaders of his day. And both the asceticism of John the Baptist and the apparent hedonism of Jesus seem to have provoked those leaders in roughly equal measure (see Matthew 11:18–19).

The sheer accessibility of Jesus' leadership is evident from the moment we first pick up a Gospel. 'Come to me,' said Jesus, and they came—synagogue rulers, royal officials, Pharisees and members of the Jewish ruling council; tax collectors, lepers, unspecified 'sinners' and women with unmentionable diseases; parents wanting Jesus to bless their little children and mothers seeking preferment for their big children; and—despite Jesus' own perception that he was 'sent only to the lost sheep of Israel' (Matthew 15:24)—Roman centurions, Samaritans, Canaanites, Greeks and some exotic visitors from the east, bearing gifts of gold, frankincense and myrrh.

Jesus' parable of the wedding banquet had it just about right: 'Go to the street corners and invite to the banquet anyone you find' (Matthew 22:9). Whatever our theology of election, Jesus appeared in no sense choosy.

Why, then, was he willing to associate with quite such mixed and frequently unsavoury company? Why was he ready to court such hostility for the stand he took on this particular issue? The answer is that accessibility lay at the very heart of the mission to which Jesus knew himself to be called. He was the Son of Man, come to seek and to save the lost. He was the shepherd called to find the sheep that had strayed. He was the doctor whose availability to the sick was integral to his sense of vocation (Luke 19:10; 15:4; Matthew 9:12). In response to his opponents, Jesus would some-times use the word 'sinner' as they did, but his own preference was to speak the non-pejorative language of lostness and disease. And for the shepherd to ignore the sheep who had strayed, or for the doctor to keep his distance from the patients who so desperately needed him, would have been the gravest dereliction of duty, the most basic disregard of the call to pastor and to heal.

There are many reasons, of course, why leaders frequently like to keep their distance. Shyness, privacy, stress, busyness: all play their part in building an invisible barrier between the leader and those who are led, while the question of leadership priorities becomes particularly acute as an organization begins to grow. But practicalities like these were not responsible for the outrage with which

Jesus' radical accessibility was greeted. Underlying that anger lay two basic values to which his opponents were variously committed: the cultivation of leadership mystique on the one hand, and the commitment to ritual purity on the other.

MISLEADERSHIP: MYSTIQUE AND RITUAL PURITY

'Mystique' was a concept that the classical world inherited from Persia (although the word itself is derived from the Latin *mysticus*). As John Adair puts it, it was the Persians who had 'introduced prostration as part of a novel method of creating an aura of divinity around their kings'.[2] This 'aura of divinity' was maintained through the remoteness of the king from his people, and found expression in the increasingly elaborate palaces, courtyards and protective walls that bedecked the ancient world. To the more dictatorial of its advocates, it could also spill over from the culture of palace to that of temple, where emperor-worship supplanted the worship of more ancient (and generally more worthwhile) deities.

Classical culture had a contrary tradition, too, in which a leader made himself accessible to his people. Xenophon, for example, found it strange that 'while every mechanic knows the tools of his trade, and the physician knows the names of all the instruments he uses, the general should be so foolish as not to know the names of the officers under him'.[3] The Greek historian Flavius Arrianus describes how the young Alexander the Great showed deep concern for the wounded after one of the battles in his Persian campaign: 'He visited them all,' writes Arrian, 'and examined their wounds, asking each man how and in what circumstances his wound was received, and allowing him to tell the story and exaggerate as much as he pleased'![4] But even Alexander, that exemplary model of motivational leadership, seems to have been progressively seduced by the Persian approach. John Adair charts his growing self-importance in later years, fuelled by flattering courtiers, both Greek and

Persian, who puffed up his pretensions to be a living god; and the drunken murder of his friend Cleitus for daring to question this doubtful development remains a significant blot on Alexander's otherwise remarkable record.

Caesar Augustus, introduced to us at the beginning of Luke's Gospel, had largely bought into the culture of 'mystique': indeed, the very name 'Augustus' ('exalted') is a simple reminder of that fact. Even the puppet-king Herod Agrippa happily received the adulation of his people ('This is the voice of a god, not of a mere mortal', Acts 12:22) and died five days later in an incident that both Luke and the Jewish historian Josephus regarded as an act of divine retribution.[5] So against this background it is hardly surprising that the accessibility of Jesus did not endear him to his Roman hearers. Jesus' words in Mark 10:42, 'Those who are regarded as rulers of the Gentiles lord it over them, and their high officials exercise authority over them', prove that he would never see eye-to-eye with his Roman contemporaries on leadership issues. Paul's later reflections also acknowledge the apparent 'foolishness' of the gospel to its Gentile hearers, not least in the kind of people whom God was gathering around the crucified carpenter: 'God chose the foolish things of the world to shame the wise' (1 Corinthians 1:27).

While mystique was part of the Roman world of Jesus' day, the Jewish culture was far more focused on the theme of ritual purity. Taking their lead from the holiness code in the Torah (and their inspiration from the great battles of the past, most especially the revolt of the Maccabees against the impurity of their Seleucid overlords[6]) and amplifying the Torah's regulations with a hundred-and-one fiddly bylaws, the Pharisees were outraged at the laxity of Jesus and the dangers of moral contagion from the company he kept. Simon the Pharisee's response to the embarrassing gate-crasher who wiped the feet of Jesus with ointment and tears is typical of this approach: 'If this man were a prophet, he would know who is touching him and what kind of woman she is—that she is a sinner' (Luke 7:39). And the beginning of that sentence—

'If this man were a prophet'—suggests that even the more sympathetic of the Pharisees regarded Jesus' radical accessibility as a major stumbling block to their acceptance of his authority as one sent by God.

Jesus' response to such criticism has already been noted, and the 'doctor' image is especially suggestive. Yes, evil can be contagious: it can infect us like yeast 'infects' a batch of dough (see Jesus' warning in Matthew 16:6). But goodness—the power of the kingdom to forgive, restore, transform and heal—is more contagious still. Jesus never underestimated the grip of sin in our lives as some more liberal commentators are prone to do: 'everyone who sins is a slave to sin', as he put it bluntly in John 8:34. Yet the Spirit's anointing to 'proclaim freedom for the prisoners and recovery of sight for the blind' (Luke 4:18) most clearly rested upon him, and with it came a completely new approach to holiness, which was proactive, not reactive; faithful, not fearful; on the front foot, not constantly in retreat. The great commission of Matthew 28 would perhaps have been fulfilled by now had only the Church emulated our Lord's example.

JESUS THE SHEPHERD

In contrast to these misleaders, Jesus' call to 'come to me' took its cue from a deep biblical image: the picture of God as shepherd alongside the 'under-shepherding' of prophet, priest and king. The good shepherd in this image was one who gathered the sheep to himself. The bad shepherd was consistently responsible for their scattering.[7]

Having bad shepherds was tantamount to having no shepherds at all, as the prophet Micaiah was bold enough to remind weak King Ahab. 'I saw all Israel scattered on the hills like sheep without a shepherd', he announced, earning for himself Ahab's grumpy response, 'Didn't I tell you that he never prophesies anything good about me, but only bad?' The context of this story is also instructive, with Ahab having gathered the people to fight the king of Aram. In the absence of a good shepherd-king (one modelled on the life of David), Micaiah warned Ahab that such attempts to gather were inappropriate. Instead Ahab should let the Israelites disperse, scatter. 'These people have no master', the prophet said. 'Let each one go home in peace' (1 Kings 22:17–18; 2 Chronicles 18:16–17).

Moving from (arguably) the worst shepherd in the Old Testament to (unarguably) the best, the most tender example of 'Come to me' leadership appears in a famous passage in Isaiah 40. There it is said of God himself, 'He tends his flock like a shepherd: he gathers the lambs in his arms and carries them close to his heart; he gently leads those that have young' (v. 11). The author of Psalm 23 also took this theme to a new level.[8] Instead of merely portraying God as the 'shepherd of Israel', the psalmist moved to a far more intimate, personal concept of the 'Lord my shepherd'. This is a shepherd who exercises (in our terms) both 'Come to me' and 'Follow me' leadership, preparing meals for the sheep and leading them along the paths of righteousness 'for his name's sake' (v. 3).

In the New Testament, this gathering imagery, in a startlingly feminine form, is a feature of Jesus' leadership in his lament over Jerusalem: 'Jerusalem, Jerusalem… how often I have longed to gather your children together, as a hen gathers her chicks under her wings, but you were not willing' (Matthew 23:37). His image of the good shepherd who 'calls his own sheep by name' (John 10:3) is similarly powerful, recalling Xenophon's critique of those generals who don't know the names of the officers under them. And Jesus didn't simply speak in such terms. Time and time again, he practised what he preached, gathering the most unlikely group of people to himself, frequently around a meal table.

The most famous 'Come to me' invitation of them all, though, is also the most illuminating. 'Come to me,' said Jesus, 'all you who are weary and burdened, and I will give you rest. Take my yoke upon you and learn from me, for I am gentle and humble in heart, and you will find rest for your souls. For my yoke is easy and my burden is light' (Matthew 11:28–30).

Many people, of course, are weary and burdened, and a hundred Christian generations have rightly found comfort in this warm and winsome invitation. But Jesus may have had a particular type of hearer in mind when he issued it—not simply those who were wearied by life in general but those who were burdened by the incessant demands of the religious leaders, with their intrusive interpretations of the law. As he said later of the Pharisees, 'They tie up heavy, cumbersome loads and put them on other people's shoulders, but they themselves are not willing to lift a finger to move them' (Matthew 23:4).

The 'yoke' of the law was later mentioned in the critical discussions of the Council of Jerusalem. In debating the question of the Church's accessibility to its growing Gentile membership, Peter wisely posed the question, 'Why do you try to test God by putting on the necks of Gentiles a yoke that neither we nor our ancestors have been able to bear?' (Acts 15:10). It's hardly surprising, then, that Jesus' gracious invitation to lay down that burden and replace it with an 'easy' yoke (perhaps in the sense of being fit for use and tailor-made for the wearer) was to prove so attractive.

It might seem ill-advised to seek to rehabilitate a much-derided children's hymn at this point. But the verse, 'Gentle Jesus, meek and mild, look upon a little child'[9] picks up some of the major traits of 'Come to me' leadership rather well, whatever its sentimental associations. Gentleness, meekness, mildness—or, to modernize the words a little, gentleness, humility and a peaceable spirit—join compassion and vulnerability as key qualities in the character of Jesus, and these virtues help to explain the radical accessibility which was to prove such a significant feature of his ministry. It is to these 'come to me' qualities that we now turn.

——— 2 ———

THE CHARACTER OF THE SHEPHERD

COMPASSION

Micaiah's phrase 'like sheep without a shepherd' had its first biblical outing in Numbers 27:17, where Moses had reflected on the need for a successor before appointing Joshua to the role, but it was also picked up by Jesus as he surveyed the huge crowds that followed him on his tour through the Galilean towns and villages. Many of those people had looked to John the Baptist for their inspiration. They had been among similarly large crowds who had converged on the Jordan River some months before, to confess, repent and receive baptism at John's hands. But now that John was in prison, they were 'harassed and helpless, like sheep without a shepherd', and Jesus' response to the situation was motivated by one single emotion: 'When he saw the crowds, he had compassion on them' (Matthew 9:36).

Being 'compassionate' involves the call to suffer with another person. The New Testament verb that it translates, *splanchnizomai*, is derived from the Greek term for innards, specifically the heart, liver and lungs—hence the somewhat earthy references to 'bowels' in the King James Bible. 'Compassion' as a noun is unheard of in the Gospels, and there may well be a reason for that. 'Having compassion' in the Jesus sense is active, energetic, motivating—not something fixed and static, a trophy attached to the pastor's wall.

There's something about the sheer gutsiness of Jesus' compassion that is deeply compelling, perfectly fleshing out the Old Testament understanding of a God who is 'gracious and compassionate, slow to anger and rich in love' (Psalm 145:8). Whether in the context of large crowds or intimate one-to-one encounters, it was Christ's compassion that motivated him to heal the sick, feed the hungry, cast out demons, raise the dead and send forth workers into the harvest field.[1] In the parable of the unmerciful servant, it was compassion that led the master to cancel his servant's debt (Matthew 18:27). In the parable of the prodigal son, it was compassion that welcomed the wretched child home (Luke 15:20).

The two great feeding miracles in the Gospels are instructive at this point (see Matthew 14:13–21; 15:29–39). In the first of them, the feeding of the five thousand, we are simply told how Jesus 'had compassion on them and healed those who were ill' (14:14). As evening approached, the disciples urged him to send the crowds away to buy food, to which Jesus responded, 'You give them something to eat' (v. 16). The resulting miracle was so remarkable as to find its place into all four Gospels.

In the subsequent feeding of the four thousand, though, the act of compassion was spelt out to the disciples (and, by implication, to us) in far greater detail. 'I have compassion for these people,' said Jesus, having gathered his disciples around him; 'they have already been with me three days and have nothing to eat. I do not want to send them away hungry, or they may collapse on the way' (Matthew 15:32). 'Because some of them have come a long distance,' adds Mark in his account of this incident (8:3).

It comes across, perhaps, as a somewhat laboured speech. Surely it should be obvious that people who've not been fed for three days need something to eat? But the reality, then and now, is that compassion is not always obvious to the followers of Jesus, and, as an elementary join-the-dots exercise in compassionate thinking, Jesus' words on this occasion could hardly be bettered.

Good shepherds, as we've seen, gather the sheep, while bad shepherds scatter them. It is ironic, then, that the very compassion of Christ would lead to a scattering of the sheep—that on the night before he died, Jesus would quote the prophecy of Zechariah 13:7: 'I will strike the shepherd, and the sheep of the flock will be scattered' (Matthew 26:31). John's account of that evening even contains echoes of Micaiah's judgment on the hapless King Ahab on the eve of his death in battle: 'A time is coming', said Jesus, 'and in fact has come when you will be scattered, each to your own home' (16:32). And the conclusion on Good Friday, as the disciples ran for their lives, seemed inevitable: Jesus' opponents had been right all along; he was a bad shepherd in the line of Ahab—a fraud, a misleader.

Yet within days, the 'God of peace' had 'brought back from the dead our Lord Jesus, that great Shepherd of the sheep' (Hebrews 13:20), and the risen Christ was in the business of gathering once again—in the garden, behind locked doors, on the road, beside the lake.

Compassion—or, rather, 'having compassion'—is at the heart of 'Come to me' leadership. It stirs, motivates and empowers, and is hugely attractive to harassed and helpless people. Compassion doesn't so much guide people along a path; rather, it draws people to a person. 'I, when I am lifted up from the earth,' said Jesus (referring again to his death, the greatest compassionate act of them all), 'will draw all people to myself' (John 12:32).

GENTLENESS

At first sight, the word 'gentleness' may seem somewhat pathetic and ineffective—for *Simpsons* enthusiasts, the defining quality of a Ned Flanders with his wife Maude and their alarmingly virtuous offspring, Rod and Todd. But *prautes*, the Greek word for 'gentleness' in the most famous of the 'Come to me' sayings (Matthew 11:28–30), is far from weak. Elsewhere in Greek literature, it is used of a wild horse being brought under control, or of a boat in a storm whose ropes and sails are harnessing the force of the wind. It means literally 'strength under control', and we see it in almost everything that Jesus did.

We might think, for example, of the time when Jesus was anointed by a 'sinner', quite probably a prostitute (Luke 7:36–39). The writer to the Hebrews teaches that Jesus was 'tempted in every way, just as we are—yet he did not sin' (4:15). That must, of course, have included sexual temptation. Yet men and women alike felt comfortable in Jesus' presence. They sensed that they could be close to him, even intimate, without risk of seduction or manipulation. For Jesus was a man with sexual feelings like the rest of humankind, but sexual feelings harnessed, brought under control—a gentle man.

Jesus' cleansing of the temple is another example of *prautes* in action—perhaps a somewhat surprising one to choose, since at face value this is hardly Jesus at his gentlest. Yet Mark reports that Jesus had visited the temple the evening before, then spent the night with his friends in Bethany before turning the tables on the money changers the following day (Mark 11:11–17). This is not the portrait of a man losing control, simply exploding at the exploitation that lay at the heart of the money changers' trade. It is the picture of a man full of righteous anger, but anger under control—a gentle man.[2]

Gethsemane is arguably the supreme instance of this 'strength under control'. There is real anguish in this story, with agonized prayer and sweat pouring off Jesus' body like drops of blood falling to the ground (Luke 22:39–44). Yet, as he rose from prayer and endured the unimaginable suffering of the following day, Jesus displayed extraordinary courage. Here was a man who could face fear in the raw but whose fear had been brought under control—a gentle man.

Strong characters frequently have the power to demolish weaker opponents. All too easily they can use their wit and charisma to make others feel very small, but Matthew's description of Jesus in terms of Isaiah's 'suffering servant' was deeply significant: 'Here is my servant whom I have chosen… A bruised reed he will not break, and a smouldering wick he will not snuff out' (12:18, 20). It reminds us of the words 'gentleman' or 'gentlewoman' used in their best possible sense—the 'verray parfit gentil knight', perhaps, of Chaucer's *Canterbury Tales*, known for his commitment to 'trouthe and honour, fredom and curteisie'.[3]

'Come to me… for I am gentle' said Jesus, and that 'strength under control' was fundamental to the quality of his leadership. For the gentle leader is a safe leader, someone who will never bully, manipulate or seduce those who are led; and the gentle leader is an enabling leader, one who will encourage and release the gifts of others without feeling threatened or exposed themselves.

HUMILITY

'Come to me…' said Jesus, 'for I am gentle and humble in heart' (Matthew 11:28–29). Gentleness (strength under control) and humility (ego under control) always go hand in hand in 'Come to me' leadership.

Humility is often identified with a lack of self-esteem and a sense of personal insignificance, a spirituality best expressed in that glorious line from an old chorus, 'We are but worms with feeble knees';[4] and the Greek word *tapeinos* (literally 'low lying'), which Jesus employs in Matthew 11, might be thought to back up this down-at-heel interpretation.

Yet true humility is far from such a pitiable attitude. It is practical, deliberate, prophetic, even provocative. It comes from a place of deep inner security, and not from a place of feebleness, weakness or underhand manipulation.

Paul makes this point as he writes (or quotes?) the magnificent hymn in Philippians 2. Christ Jesus was 'in very nature God', writes Paul, but deliberately 'made himself nothing, taking the very nature of a servant… And being found in appearance as a man, he humbled himself and became obedient to death—even death on a cross' (vv. 6–8, NIV). Jesus' time on earth may have been 'low-lying', but only because of his deliberate commitment to downward mobility for the sake of fallen humanity.

'Therefore God exalted him to the highest place', the hymn continues, 'and gave him the name that is above every name' (v. 9). For only the humble can be entrusted with positions of authority, as the New Testament consistently reiterates[5]—and the greater the humility, the higher the authority. In J.C. Ryle's challenging words (relating to us, not to Jesus), 'Most of Christ's labourers probably have as much success as their souls can bear.'[6]

It is in John's description of the 'night before he died' that this theme is dramatically expressed in the form of a moving enacted parable (13:1–17). Jesus, we are told, 'knew that the Father had put all things under his power, and that he had come from God and was returning to God' (v. 3)—certainly no lack of personal significance here! Yet from that place of inner security he was able to stoop down to the level of his disciples' feet, making himself a servant on their behalf.

The scene is not difficult to imagine: Jesus' disciples sitting around the table, starting the meal with those feet still dirty. There was clearly a sense of awkwardness in the air, the disciples perhaps pretending to ignore the social blunder. We know from the other Gospels that there had recently been a childish dispute between them about who was the greatest (Mark 10:35–45), so any idea that one of the disciples might humiliate himself in front of his peers was virtually inconceivable. And the result—as is inevitably the case when pride is involved—was stalemate. No one moved because to move would be to express subservience.

So Jesus moved. He 'took off' his outer clothing (the word literally means 'laid aside', just as the good shepherd in John 10:11 lays aside his life for the sheep); he poured water into a basin and calmly started to wash his disciples' feet.

In normal circumstances, a foot-washing slave would have been completely invisible: he would not have been thanked, applauded or noticed at all. On this occasion, though, every eye was on Jesus: every uncomfortable, embarrassed face turned towards him. For here were men learning a lesson in humility, a lesson that would prove both fundamental and revolutionary. Here were men learning that true humility is not weakness. It is rather strength—the strength of those who don't need to show off or worry about their position among their peers, because theirs is a calm, inner security that makes human power games look shabby and childish by comparison.

Simon Peter was later to write in his first letter, 'Clothe yourselves with humility towards one another, because "God opposes the proud but shows favour to the humble"' (1 Peter 5:5). And it's significant that this exhortation was directed specifically towards the 'young men' among his readers—young men like the Twelve, jockeying for position around the table in the upper room.

Humility, then, is another key characteristic of Jesus' 'Come to me' leadership. A lack of humility leads to stalemate in our relationship with God, where our self-sufficiency keeps him effectively at arm's length, and stalemate in our relationship with others, where the desire to maintain our dignity and justify our every action blocks us off from all warm, meaningful, genuinely human contact. A proud individual can still notch up the odd success, primarily through coercion or manipulation, but the personal cost of such achievements is far too high. In Jesus' pithy epigram, 'What good will it be for you to gain the whole world, yet forfeit your soul?' (Matthew 16:26).

A PEACEABLE SPIRIT

Compassion, gentleness, humility—but what of the 'mildness' reflected in that hymn, 'Gentle Jesus, meek and mild'? In the 18th century, when Charles Wesley wrote these words, it meant someone who was peaceable, conciliatory—a man or woman who, in Paul's words, makes 'every effort to keep the unity of the Spirit through the bond of peace' (Ephesians 4:3).

Jesus' experience in three years of public ministry was hardly 'mild' or 'peaceable' in the normal sense. The constant carping of the Pharisees and Sadducees; the rejection by the people of his home town who, within weeks of his baptism, were seeking to throw him off a cliff (Luke 4:28–29); the confusion of his brothers, who 'did not believe in him' (John 7:5) and considered him 'out of his mind' (Mark 3:21)—all led him to recognize that any superficial talk of 'peace, peace, where there is no peace' was just as inappropriate as in the day of Jeremiah the prophet (see Jeremiah 6:14). 'I did not come to bring peace, but a sword', as he put it in one of the toughest of the Gospel passages: 'your enemies will be the members of your own household' (Matthew 10:34, 36). It may not have been intentional, but it was certainly predictable that families, villages and the whole religious establishment would be divided over a ministry in which neutrality was simply not an option.

Yet Jesus was in no sense someone who relished a fight. As he walked towards Jerusalem on the way to his death, he gave us two insights into his real feelings about the city. The first, to which we have already referred, portrayed Jesus as not so much the good shepherd as the good chicken: 'Jerusalem, Jerusalem, you who kill the prophets and stone those sent to you, how often I have longed to gather your children together, as a hen gathers her chicks under her wings, but you were not willing' (Luke 13:34). The second expressed stronger emotions still: 'As he approached Jerusalem and saw the city', writes Luke, 'he wept over it and said, "If you, even you, had only known on this day what would bring you peace—but now it is hidden from your eyes"' (19:41–42).

The tears of Jesus (today commemorated in the beautiful teardrop shape of the church of Dominus Flevit on the Mount of Olives) were in part a response to the disaster that he predicted for Jerusalem, a prophecy fulfilled in the appalling siege of the city in AD70, but the root of this disaster lay deeper still. The name Jerusalem means literally 'city of peace', yet its inhabitants seemed blind to the peace that God was offering them, and deaf to the song of the angels with its promise of 'peace on earth' (Luke 2:14). 'You did not recognize the time of God's coming to you' (19:44), Jesus sadly concluded, at the beginning of a week in which the rapturous applause of the triumphal entry would degenerate into the angry cries of 'Crucify him! Crucify him!'

If Jesus proved unwilling to proclaim 'Peace, peace, where there is no peace', there is no question of his commitment to create a peaceful community—and to do so out of the most diverse and unpromising material, as his disciples jostled for position and Matthew (the Roman collaborator) daily broke bread with Simon (the Zealot). Peter probably saw himself as the good boy in the class when he asked the question, 'Lord, how many times shall I forgive someone who sins against me? Up to seven times?' (Matthew 18:21). Seven times must have appeared pretty generous on the whole, but Jesus' answer was far more realistic, especially in the context of the communal lifestyle to which he was calling them: 'I tell you, not seven times, but seventy times seven!' (v. 22).

It was in the upper room that this peaceable vision was most powerfully expressed. John's account of that evening gives us four solid chapters of teaching following the foot-washing incident— teaching that culminated in Jesus' moving prayer for the unity of his disciples, a unity founded on nothing less than the inseparable oneness of Father and Son. 'Holy Father, protect them by the power of your name—the name you gave me—so that they may be one as we are one', prayed Jesus (17:11), and the subsequent verses make it clear that this prayer was far-reaching and universal, a plea for all future believers, not simply the apostolic band.

Such a unified community would be a 'good and pleasant' place to belong to, as the writer of Psalm 133 recognizes in his freeflowing rhapsody on the subject, but Jesus' vision was far broader and more mission-oriented than that. True unity was such a rare commodity in his day (as in ours) that a reconciled messianic community, infused by the Spirit of God, was bound to make its mark: 'May they be brought to complete unity to let the world know that you sent me and have loved them even as you have loved me' (John 17:23, NIV).

Luke gives us an idea of what that community might look like, in his two little portraits of the post-Pentecost church (Acts 2:42–47; 4:32–37). Alongside descriptions of shared goods and possessions, miraculous signs and wonders and a depth of fellowship that is truly inspiring, he makes the missionary comment, 'And the Lord added to their number daily those who were being saved' (2:47). It is not simply that the early Church had staked its pitch in the largest public space in central Jerusalem—the temple courts—though that was unquestionably a sound strategy. Nor is it simply that the wind of the Spirit was blowing with extraordinary strength and vigour in the immediate aftermath of Pentecost. It was the sheer quality of their life together—guided by generosity and freedom, not by some formalized community rule—that made the early Church quite so attractive and the gospel quite so contagious.

And 'Come to me' leadership always has that dimension. Like a hen gathering the chicks under her wings, the 'Come to me' leader will look to gather, to unite, to hold together the frequently squabbling members of the family in a communal oneness that would be completely unsustainable without the empowering Spirit of Jesus.

'Come to me' leadership even has a somewhat matriarchal feel about it. It reminds us perhaps of the assiduous grandmother who makes it her life's mission to keep in touch with the family—and, equally importantly, to keep her family in touch and at peace with one another. And perhaps it was the very diversity of the community that Jesus gathered under his wing that made (and still makes) the call to unity both so urgent and so extraordinarily difficult. A community of the like-minded is comparatively easy to hold together; a community of the diverse is a far more challenging prospect. That challenge continues to provide a running theme (sometimes a running sore) in the book of Acts, in Paul's letters, and through the entire history of the Church.

VULNERABILITY

'Come to me': thus far the invitation has been focused on the need of the hearer, not of the caller, but there are times when the situation is reversed—when the caller, rather than the hearer, is the one in need.

The 'Follow me' leader can avoid such occasions entirely: a proper distance is observed between leader and led, and a 'stiff upper lip' becomes the order of the day. But the moment a leader dares to say,

'I no longer call you servants... I have called you friends' (John 15:15), there is a step-change in the leadership dynamic. Interdependence replaces dependence, accessibility becomes a two-way path, and from that point there is no turning back.

The Gospel writers consistently refused to portray Jesus in the glamorous light of the later Docetists,[7] as some kind of immaculate creature floating several feet off the ground, immune from the trials and tribulations of ordinary mortals. In the Gospel records we have a Jesus who rejoices and weeps, a Jesus who is hungry, thirsty, sweaty and tired, a Jesus who is powerless at his birth and equally powerless in his dying. When you abandon this Jesus, he is lonely. When you cut this Jesus, he bleeds.

There is what we might call an 'objective vulnerability' at the heart of these portraits. The incarnation is a full-blooded reality, not a moderately convincing attempt at divine role-play. But the Gospels also portray Jesus as vulnerable in a more subjective sense, choosing to open himself to those around him. In the early part of John's Gospel we are told how Jesus 'would not entrust himself' to the crowd, because he 'knew all people' (John 2:24)—words that demonstrate a carefulness, a natural reticence on Jesus' part. As trust developed between Jesus and his disciples, though—as they moved from being his servants to becoming his friends, and especially as the cross cast a deeper over the latter stages of his ministry—so Jesus increasingly revealed his feelings to those who were closest to him.

Jesus knew and loved the Psalms, that rich selection of poems and meditations that collectively made up the Jewish hymnal; and the Psalms run the whole gamut of human emotions, as their writers moved from the deepest and darkest of valleys to the highest and most wondrous of mountain tops. Joy and celebration take their place beside tougher, more troubling emotions—anger, envy, anxiety, frustration, sorrow, abandonment and despair.

Sometimes the psalmist's vulnerability is expressed with the benefit of hindsight: 'I sought the Lord, and he answered me: he delivered me from all my fears' (Psalm 34:4). Such reflections are right and proper, looking back on the faithfulness of God and praising him for coming through at just the right moment. Sometimes, though, it comes straight from the heart—in that harrowing cry of Psalm 22:1, for example: 'My God, my God, why have you forsaken me?' The Psalms were among the best of the spiritual heritage that shaped Jesus' own understanding, so it's not surprising to find him alluding to them on numerous occasions.

Processed vulnerability—vulnerability with the benefit of hindsight—may be edifying but it is also pretty safe. It's not so difficult to stand up in front of a congregation and say with King David, '[God] lifted me out of the slimy pit, out of the mud and mire; he set my feet on a rock and gave me a firm place to stand' (Psalm 40:2). But the unsettling thing about Jesus' vulnerability was how often he seemed to specialize in the unprocessed, raw variety.

Jesus wept over Jerusalem; he wept at the tomb of Lazarus, his friend. He also praised God enthusiastically as one 'full of joy through the Holy Spirit' (Luke 10:21), and both actions—anguished weeping and exuberant joy—tend to be equally embarrassing from an Anglo-Saxon perspective. Jesus asked a Samaritan woman for a drink, even when he knew full well that 'Jews do not associate with Samaritans' (John 4:9). He accepted the anointing of his feet by a fallen woman who had 'done a beautiful thing to me' (Matthew 26:10). We've touched on the garden of Gethsemane already, but Jesus' openness to his disciples there—'My soul is overwhelmed with sorrow to the point of death'—is matched with the most needy of requests: 'Stay here and keep watch with me' (Matthew 26:38); and when he took up the anguished cry of Psalm 22 as he hung on the cross in the darkness, this was vulnerability at its rawest, its most unrefined.

Compassion, gentleness, humility, a peaceable spirit, vulnerability: these qualities lie at the heart of the unique accessibility that was such a striking feature of Jesus' leadership. Yet what was the source of those qualities? And how did Jesus maintain his 'Come to me' appeal in the midst of such a busy and demanding ministry?

✠

——— 3 ———

JESUS' ACCESS TO THE FATHER

The Introduction to this book brought forward the idea of Jesus as the perfect disciple, and as we read the Gospels one thing becomes clear—that Jesus' accessibility to his followers was firmly founded on the Father's accessibility to Jesus. Time and again we see Jesus withdrawing to a solitary place to commune with God (see Matthew 14:13; Mark 1:35). On the odd occasion, we're even given a privileged glimpse into the very nature of that communion (especially in the Gospel accounts of events in the garden of Gethsemane), and, although scholarly opinion is divided on the exact meaning of the Aramaic word *Abba*,[1] there's no question that the intimacy of Jesus' relationship with his Father was foundational to his life, his ministry and his extraordinary accessibility as a 'Come to me' leader.

Perhaps this point is best made in relation to the most famous 'Come to me' passage of all, for Matthew 11 gives us one of those privileged insights into the nature of Jesus' prayer life and the root of his accessibility to those around him. In a passage strongly reminiscent of John's Gospel, Jesus starts praying with the words, 'I praise you, Father, Lord of heaven and earth, because you have hidden these things from the wise and learned, and revealed them to little children. Yes, Father, for this was your good pleasure' (vv. 25–26). Then follows a remarkable paragraph that sounds as if it could have come straight out of John: 'All things have been committed to me by my Father. No one knows the Son except the Father, and no one knows the Father except the Son and those to whom the Son chooses to reveal him' (v. 27). Finally, off the back of these profound reflections, Jesus issues the famous invitation: 'Come to me, all you who are weary and burdened, and I will give you rest' (v. 28).

Matthew's account here portrays the close intimacy of Jesus' relationship with his Father before recording his invitation to the weary and burdened. The source of Jesus' 'Come to me' qualities—compassion, humility, vulnerability and so on—is to be found in the solitary place where he communes with his Father, with Abba.

Jesus himself drew great inspiration at this point from the person of Moses, one of the undisputed giants in the history of Israel. For despite his impressive upbringing in the Pharaoh's court, and a rather hot-headed incident in his early adulthood (see Exodus 2:11–12), Moses comes across as a sympathetic and gentle man, though not afraid to confront immorality or injustice whenever he saw it.

In Exodus 3 and 4 (the famous close encounter at the burning bush), Moses' vulnerability is clearly revealed in a series of anxious responses: 'Who am I, that I should go to Pharaoh and bring the Israelites out of Egypt? … What if they do not believe me or listen to me? … O Lord, I have never been eloquent… I am slow of speech and tongue… O Lord, please send someone else to do it' (3:11; 4:1, 10, 13).

In Numbers 12, at a time when Moses was somewhat more comfortable in his leadership role, the writer comments, 'Now Moses was a very humble man, more humble than anyone else on the face of the earth' (v. 3).

Also, in Exodus 18, we have the picture of a man who has simply become too accessible, and needs his father-in-law, Jethro, to sort him out: 'When his father-in-law saw all that Moses was doing for the people, he said, "What is this you are doing for the people? Why do you alone sit as judge, while all these people stand around you from morning till evening? … What you are doing is not good. You and these people who come to you will only wear yourselves out" (vv. 14, 17–18).[2] It often takes someone in Jethro's position to make comments of this kind (especially if they feel that their beloved daughter and grandchildren are being neglected by a workaholic son-in-law), and Jethro's sound advice led to one of the earliest and most impressive examples of delegation in the history of Israel.

There was one place, however, where Moses could never be reached: a small tent outside the Israelite camp, which he named the 'tent of meeting'. (This was a more informal place than the tabernacle, also confusingly called the 'Tent of Meeting', which was even then being constructed in the centre of the camp.) The crowds gathered round this place but only Moses was allowed inside, with Joshua acting as a kind of holy bouncer on his behalf, and in that place of sanctuary, we read, 'The Lord would speak to Moses face to face, as one speaks to a friend' (33:11).

There's an element of mystique surrounding Moses' close encounters with the divine. On one occasion we are told how the people were 'afraid to come near him' because of the brilliant radiance of his face (Exodus 34:30)—a problem that was only partially resolved through the judicious wearing of a veil (v. 33).[3] The overall picture, though, is of a man whose early experience as a shepherd equipped him for a ministry that was both pastoral and relational. 'Come to me', as we've seen, speaks of a face-to-face encounter, and as the Lord spoke to Moses face to face, so Moses in turn grew in the humility and approachability of a supremely gifted 'Come to me' leader.

Jesus, then, had an excellent role model in the person of Moses and in his divine encounters in the tent of meeting. We find echoes of the Exodus verses in John 15, where Jesus speaks to his disciples face to face in the upper room and calls them his friends. 'When you pray,' said Jesus in the Sermon on the Mount, 'go into your room, close the door and pray to your Father, who is unseen. Then your Father, who sees what is done in secret, will reward you' (Matthew 6:6). Quietness, privacy, friendship, a one-to-one encounter: these seem to have been central to the devotional life of Jesus, and to the lives of the apostles, who in turn recognized their twin calling to 'prayer and the ministry of the word' (Acts 6:4).

By contrast, the misleaders to whom we have already been introduced—those who cultivated a leadership mystique and those who emphasized ritual purity—had little time for a humbling face-to-face encounter with the Almighty. The Gospels give us few insights into the worship life of the pagans of the day, although Jesus does warn his followers, 'Do not keep on babbling like pagans, for they think they will be heard because of their many words' (Matthew 6:7). Pagan religion, it seems, hadn't moved on much since the days of Elijah, when the prophets of Baal famously pranced round their sacrifices from morning to night, shouting and prophesying and cutting themselves with swords and spears (1 Kings 18). But the devotional life of the Jewish misleaders is mentioned on rather more occasions—most notably, again, in the Sermon on the Mount and in Jesus' scathing criticism of the Pharisees in Matthew 23.

'When you pray, do not be like the hypocrites', said Jesus in Matthew 6:5, 'for they love to pray standing in the synagogues and on the street corners to be seen by others.' The tent of meeting had been replaced by a street corner. Quietness and privacy had been traded for noise and bustle. The face-to-face encounter with God had been exchanged for a pathetic attempt to win human praise. It's hardly surprising, in such a context, that the humility and approachability of Moses had been supplanted by the pride and haughtiness of those who sat 'in Moses' seat' (23:2).

Even the temple seems to have become a place where piety was paraded and Pharisees engaged in self-congratulatory prayers. Jesus' parable of the Pharisee and the tax collector may have an element of caricature in it—but caricatures only work because of the sharp element of truth that they contain. 'God, I thank you that I am not like other people—robbers, evildoers, adulterers—or even like this tax collector. I fast twice a week and give a tenth of all I get' (Luke 18:11–12). It's instructive that the Pharisee's brief prayer mentions himself four times and God only once. Prayer is supposed to be a window between earth and heaven. In the Pharisee's case, it was more like a mirror.

There's a telling phrase in Luke's Gospel, which goes some way in explaining the heart of the Pharisees' misleadership: 'The Pharisees and the experts in the law rejected God's purpose for themselves, because they had not been baptized by John' (7:30). Not having responded to John's challenge, or to the humility and vulnerability involved in his call to baptism, it was inevitable that these misleaders should have been unprepared for the coming of the Messiah, too self-important and self-absorbed to see beyond their own insatiable need for approval.

Here, then, is the heart of the 'Come to me' leadership of Jesus. It was in his 'tent of meeting', in the solitary place, 'in my Father's house' (Luke 2:49), that Jesus' character was developed and his unique accessibility forged. Such an example is both inspiring and illuminating and has considerable implications for Christian living and leadership today. For accessibility remains a key value for all who seek to lead a team that is encouraged, motivated and personally committed to the task in hand.

✠

——— 4 ———

LIVING WITHIN EASY REACH

There were 30 candidates for baptism that day—all adults, all brand new Christian believers and each of them delighted to be expressing their faith in an open-air act of witness; and as Pastor Sasha and I waded into the lake, a sense of the great privilege of what we were about to do swept over me. The setting was the east of Ukraine, an area that, until very recently, had been part of the Soviet empire, where such meetings would have been illegal. The lake was surrounded by a beach on which members of the church were gathered, alongside a variety of swimmers, paddlers and sunbathers. Someone started up a hymn and was quickly joined by other singers, many of them effortlessly harmonizing the tune or adding little descants of their own.

Then, one by one, the 30 candidates stripped down to T-shirts and shorts and stepped somewhat gingerly into the lake. All were baptized (in both English and Ukrainian), then returned to the bank, where they were received with hugs and kisses and warm applause. A white robe was placed on them—a symbol of their new life in Christ—and a simple meal was shared. Having attracted the attention of most of the sunbathers and swimmers, an impromptu evangelistic event was held there on the beach as Pastor Sasha wasted no time in drawing together potential candidates for his next baptismal service.

The five 'Come to me' qualities of the last chapter—or some very like them—are applauded in many places in the New Testament. In the Beatitudes, the meek inherit the earth, mourners are comforted, the merciful are shown mercy and peacemakers are called children of God (Matthew 5:1–11). In the early chapters of Acts, we see precisely these qualities lived out by the first Christian community. In Philippians 4, Paul writes: 'Let your gentleness be evident to all' (v. 5). In his first epistle, John speaks of the *agape* love that expresses itself in practical compassion to 'a brother or sister in need' (1 John 3:17).

Paul's first letter to the Thessalonians is full of 'Come to me' warmth. 'As apostles of Christ', he writes, 'we could have been a burden to you, but we were gentle among you, like a mother caring for her little children' (2:6–7, NIV). And the next sentence summarizes the theme almost better than anything else: 'We loved you so much that we were delighted to share with you not only the gospel of God but our lives as well, because you had become so dear to us' (v. 8, NIV).

Yet as I helped to baptize those 30 candidates in a Ukrainian lake, it was another verse that came to mind: 'Therefore, as God's chosen people, holy and dearly loved, clothe yourselves with compassion, kindness, humility, gentleness and patience' (Colossians 3:12). A little earlier in the letter, Paul had called on his readers to 'put to death... whatever belongs to your earthly nature' (v. 5), and had listed some of the old 'clothes' that fitted them in their prebaptismal lives. But now, he wrote, they were to be dressed with nothing other than the character of Christ himself: the 'Come to me' qualities of compassion, gentleness, humility, along with the love 'which binds them all together in perfect unity' (v. 14).

The language of 'clothing ourselves' is deceptively simple. Other than the tying of bow-ties (which I've always found an extraordinarily challenging exercise), most people learn how to get dressed at a very early age. How, though, do we clothe ourselves with compassion or humility? How do we grow in gentleness or in an appropriate vulnerability? These are questions that every Christian should be asking as they seek to put on the likeness of Christ—questions that are especially foundational for all those called to 'Come to me' leadership.

Paul never said it, of course—and perhaps it's dangerous to put words in his mouth—but just as he wrote, 'Follow my example, as I follow the example of Christ', might he not have approved of another sentiment: 'Come to me, as I come to Christ'? The apostle Andrew and an unnamed disciple were privileged to come to Christ at the beginning of John's Gospel: 'They went and saw where he was staying, and they spent that day with him' (1:39). Mary of Bethany chose 'what is better' by sitting at Jesus' feet and listening to what he said (Luke 10:42). But what of that chilling scenario in Matthew 7, where a group of people appear before Jesus at the end of time and smugly remind him how they've prophesied in his name and cast out demons and performed many miracles, only to be told, 'I never knew you. Away from me, you evildoers!' (vv. 21–23)?

'They spent that day with him'; she 'has chosen what is better'; 'I never knew you': all three phrases point to the need for us to find that 'tent of meeting', that encounter with the living God, if we are to be transformed into his likeness and so become genuinely accessible to the people around us.

THE SEDUCTIVENESS OF INACCESSIBILITY

Before we explore the 'tent of meeting', though, it is important to face up to one or two home truths. It's easy to respond to the parable of the Pharisee and the tax collector (Luke 18:9–14) with the prayer, 'God, I thank you that I am not like that Pharisee!' but the reality is that misleadership is extraordinarily prevalent today—misleadership based on an arrogant refusal to do business with the true God.

The cultivation of leadership mystique takes many forms, and the string of dictators who so defaced the history of our planet in the 20th century (and those who continue to do so today) are a salutary reminder that the emperor cult is far from dead and buried. For most people, though, the temptation is far less grandiose and therefore much more difficult to spot. Pedestals can be built from many different materials. They can be erected very slowly over the course of decades or be put up at great speed by a community hungry for heroes. They can take the form of a self-build package or can be constructed without the knowledge or consent of those who are placed upon them. And as the pedestal grows higher and higher, so the person upon it becomes more inaccessible, more remote, more lonely, with an ever increasing distance to fall when it all goes wrong.

It is possible to build a pedestal through the judicious use of lies and propaganda, but far more common is the temptation to be selectively truthful—to tell the truth and nothing but the truth, but not to tell the whole truth in our self-disclosure to those around us. One day, for example, I could write a book about my life based on the various miraculous events that I have been privileged to witness. Such a book might sell well and establish my reputation as a man who walks from one miracle to the next—an account which is at the same time entirely truthful and deeply misleading. The reality of Christian living is generally fairly ordinary (for me as, I suppose, for many others), though punctuated by the odd event that reminds me of the power of the God who has graciously called us into his service.

One of the best writers on this theme is Eugene Peterson, whose book *The Gift* focuses on another classic pedestal commonly built for, or by, Christian people and especially their leaders—the reputation for busyness that keeps others at arm's length and creates an aura of commitment, importance and self-sacrifice. Peterson writes:

The one piece of mail certain to go unread into my waste-basket is the letter addressed to the 'busy pastor'. I'm not arguing the accuracy of the adjective; I am, though, contesting the way it's used to flatter and express sympathy.

'This poor man', we say. 'He's so devoted to his flock; the work is endless, and he sacrifices himself so unstintingly.' But the word 'busy' is the symptom not of commitment but of betrayal. The adjective 'busy' set

as a modifier to 'pastor' should sound to our ears like 'adulterous' to characterise a wife or 'embezzling' to describe a banker. It is an outrageous scandal, a blasphemous affront.[1]

Peterson is certainly not advocating idleness in his description of the glories of a pastoral ministry that is 'unbusy'. The calling of the Christian leader, as we shall see in Part Two, frequently involves hard work and sacrifice. He is reminding us, though, of the need for space to 'learn quietness and attentiveness before God'[2] and, above all, of the need to resist the building of a particularly insidious pedestal. The flattery that dangerously moulded the self-image of Alexander the Great remains a force to be reckoned with in the far more ordinary context of our day-to-day ministry.

Mystique was characteristic of much of the leadership of the ancient world and remains so today, but its counterpart, ritual purity, is also an enduring temptation, though again in a modified form.

It is quite natural for men and women to gather together with others who share their interests, their values, their intellect and even their dress sense. It is quite natural for groups to form, with some people within the group, others outside the group and still others who don't quite know where they belong. The distinctiveness of different cultures depends on such universal human behaviour.

There is a problem here, though, as the Pharisees' commitment to ritual purity so clearly demonstrates—that such cultures can all too easily become exclusive, detached, judgmental and ultimately compromised. If my culture remains unchallenged—if I simply surround myself with others who think as I do—then the sins and shortcomings of that culture will continue unchecked. I will become horribly adept at pointing out the specks in the eyes of those outside my culture while remaining oblivious to the logs wedged in the eyes of those within it—of whom I myself may well be the most deluded of all.

Jesus' ability to be the best possible example of the Jewish culture of his day while simultaneously remaining accessible to those whose behaviour so scandalized his religious contemporaries demonstrates the gospel response to this cultural conundrum. Jesus never lapsed into moral relativism: he never failed to call sin 'sin', even when it was committed by a woman at her most threatened and vulnerable (John 8:2–11). Yet he did open himself to many whose cultures and lifestyle choices were radically different from his own, and could even use the morality of those cultures to challenge the short-comings of the straitlaced pharisaical ethos that prided itself on its purity and godliness.[3]

For many Christians—and especially, perhaps, for church leaders —this can pose an uncomfortable challenge. It's all too easy to live in a bubble, surrounded by Christian believers who are just like us. Under the guise of 'fellowship', such a bubble might seem to represent God's will for our lives. Under the label of 'pastor', such a bubble might be equally justified. 'Our job,' as one senior clergy-man put it to me, 'is to feed sheep, not to entertain goats.'

This is an area, though, where the metaphor of sheep and goats begins to break down, for people are people, and every 'goat' is a potential 'sheep'. If we remain inaccessible to those outside the flock, it is not just that our Christian subculture will remain unchallenged (with all the dangers of exclusiveness, judgmentalism and compromise that that implies). It is also that the chance for goats to become sheep, for the sick to be healed and the lost to be found, is fatally undermined. 'Come to me' leadership in Jesus' sense must be an open invitation or it's no invitation at all.

How can God deal with our various attempts to distance our-selves from other people, to stand proudly on our pedestals or quietly pass by on the other side? He can do so only if we regularly draw close to him in that private one-to-one encounter where our pride is exposed for the ridiculous thing it is, and where we are clothed afresh with the 'Come to me' qualities of compassion, gentleness, humility and love.

THE TENT OF MEETING

For Moses it was a tent; for Jesus it was a 'solitary place'; for Elijah it was a mountaintop; for the author of Psalm 84 it was the 'courts of the Lord', and many Christians today have a preferred space into which they come with real expectation of an encounter with God.

Of course, 'the earth is the Lord's, and everything in it,' as Psalm 24:1 puts it. 'The world is charged with the grandeur of God,' writes Gerard Manley Hopkins and, in the most famous verse from 'Aurora Leigh', Elizabeth Barrett Browning tells us:

> *Earth's crammed with heaven*
> *and every common bush afire with God,*
> *but only he who sees takes off his shoes;*
> *the rest sit round and pluck blackberries.*

The potential is there in all of creation to be a tent of meeting, in which the Lord might speak to us 'face to face, as one speaks to a friend' (Exodus 33:11). Yet there is something in the human psyche that needs to set apart a place to do business with the Almighty: a place that is holy both in a general way (for if 'the earth is the Lord's', then all space is holy), but is also 'sanctified' in a more specific and personal sense. This space may mean very little to other people—it may look like a rather scruffy tent with very little to commend it—but for us it is imbued with a sense of expectation, for here we come to meet with God.

John Stott helpfully lays the theological grounds for this encounter in his book *The Cross of Christ*. 'Access,' he says, 'is another blessing of reconciliation. It seems to denote the active communion with God, especially in prayer, which his reconciled children enjoy.'[4]

Stott quotes from Ephesians 2, where Paul writes to the Gentiles in the church, reminding them of how 'you who once were far away have been brought near through the blood of Christ' (v. 13).

The epistle continues by reflecting on the theme of reconciliation between human beings, especially in the context of the vexed relationship between Jew and Gentile: 'For [Christ] himself is our peace, who has made the two one and has destroyed the barrier, the dividing wall of hostility… He came and preached peace to you who were far away and peace to those who were near. For through him we both have access to the Father by the one Spirit' (vv. 14, 17–18).

Our accessibility towards one another is once again seen to be founded on God's accessibility towards us. As we come into the presence of the crucified and risen Christ—as together we enter our 'tent of meeting'—so we recognize afresh how the 'wall of hostility' has been pulled down, and all that remains is a renewed humility, compassion and openness towards one another. And this is not only true of Jew and Gentile. It is true of all strained relationships, from the harshest of tribal conflicts to the mildest of marital tiffs. Human attempts to find common ground may have some value but, time and again, the true breakthroughs occur in the tent of meeting, where Christ issues the invitation, 'Come to me… and I will give you rest' and we respond with a sense of humbled relief.

How do we go about choosing such places? In many ways they are chosen for us by our personalities, our past experiences and the church traditions in which we are nurtured. If I meet with God at a large charismatic conference, I will return to that conference the following year with a barely concealed feeling of excitement and an openness to a fresh encounter. If my tent of meeting is a particular mountain or a much-loved church building or a room in my house, it is there that I will come with a genuine sense of expectation.

Activities, as much as geographical locations, may constitute tents of meeting. For many, the daily Eucharist will be at the heart of their spirituality. For others, it will be the so-called 'quiet time', complete with extemporary prayer and a systematic reading of the scriptures. Hymns or more informal worship songs have a great ability to draw us into a conscious awareness of the presence of

God. Great works of art or music or literature, particular prayers or poems or icons: all have potential as tents of meeting, places made holy by the potent combination of the presence of God and the hope-filled anticipation of those made in his image. Even our working environment can become a meeting place, as Brother Lawrence famously discovered among the pots and pans of his Carmelite monastery kitchen: 'I possess God as peacefully in the bustle of my kitchen, where sometimes several people are asking me for different things at the same time, as I do upon my knees before the Holy Sacrament... I turn my little omelette in the pan for the love of God.'[5]

There are dangers here, of course. The history of the human race demonstrates an extraordinary capacity for idolatry—for worshipping the most unlikely of creatures and the strangest of artefacts—and the Bible's consistent warning against serving 'created things rather than the Creator' (Romans 1:25) rightly checks our enthusiasm to imbue the tent itself with mystical significance or superstitious power. Even the Eucharist or the quiet time can become a stumbling block, a ritualistic end in itself rather than a meeting place with the Almighty. Even prayer can become idolatrous in an age where more people admit to praying than to believing in God. 'The power of prayer' may be convenient shorthand, but it's also deeply misleading. Prayer itself is completely powerless; prayer never changed anything. It is the living God who is all-powerful and who frequently chooses to exercise that power in response to our praying.

Whatever the dangers, though, the human need for holy places remains, and it is vitally important that we make regular time and space to enter consciously into the presence of God if we are to be clothed with humility and compassion, and be truly accessible to those around us.

What happens when we approach our tent, perhaps with genuine hope and longing, and the place seems empty and deserted —when, like Lucy and her siblings in C.S. Lewis's story, we enter the wardrobe and discover that it has a wooden back, like any other wardrobe, and the way to Narnia is blocked?[6] The author of Psalm 42 clearly had that experience: he reflects on 'how I used to go to the house of God… with shouts of joy and praise among the festive throng' but how those days now seem light years away. 'My tears have been my food day and night,' he complains. 'When can I go and meet with God?' (vv. 2–4).

There is an argument for continuing to enter the tent of meeting whether we feel like it or not. Our feelings come and go, and may therefore need to be supplemented with a good dose of discipline when times are hard. But the psalmist's dilemma is also suggestive of a more radical solution, which is to explore different tents of meeting, those outside our own tradition or natural inclination. My tent may have become too comfortable and unadventurous, too tailor-made for my own limited self, too lacking in spiritual reality, warmth or challenge. Maybe God is calling me to be a pilgrim for a while, to explore the quieter tents of a more contemplative spirituality or the noisier tents of a faith that sings and dances with the energy and vitality of the living God.

Richard Foster has been a source of inspiration to many, calling Christians (especially evangelical Christians) back to the classical disciplines of meditation, prayer, fasting and solitude, and encouraging the exploration of a variety of tents of meeting.[7] In his excellent book *Streams of Living Water* he writes of how 'God is bringing together streams of life that have been isolated from one another for a very long time'. He continues:

This isolation is completely understandable from a historical perspective. Over the centuries some precious teaching or vital experience is neglected until, at the appropriate moment, a person or movement arises to correct the omission. Numbers of people come under the renewed teaching, but soon vested interests and a host of other factors come into play, producing resistance to the renewal, and the new movement is denounced. In time it forms its own structures and community life, often in isolation from other Christian communities.[8]

Foster goes on to identify six of these traditions, each of them flowing from the character and practice of Jesus himself, and to encourage a generosity towards one another which is able to learn rather than judge or criticize. My tent may be a good place to be (to replace Foster's metaphor with my own), but a confident faith remains genuinely receptive to the riches of other tents in which fellow believers have encountered God for themselves.

Bill Hybels' definition of character has already been quoted ('who you are when no-one is looking') but a vital aspect of the growth of our characters lies rather in 'where you are when no-one is looking' —the time spent in our tent of meeting, where veils are removed and we are progressively transformed through our encounter with God.[9] Such time may seem wasted to those concerned with high productivity and 'getting things done'. Such transformation may seem so painfully slow as to be virtually negligible. Even pastors are constantly tempted to neglect an activity whose effectiveness is so hard to assess, compared with the obvious achievement of writing a sermon or answering 100 emails.

Yet although our time in the tent is largely unseen by those around us, the growth of a relationship with one who astonishingly calls us his 'friends' remains our first and most joyful calling. As Jesus says in John 17:3, 'This is eternal life: that they know you, the only true God, and Jesus Christ, whom you have sent.'

Being caught up in ceaseless activity—even godly activity—is a trap rather than an achievement, earning for ourselves not divine congratulation but some of the saddest words from the lips of Jesus: 'I never knew you' (Matthew 7:23). Such a lifestyle also isolates us from those we are called to love, as our distance from God makes us far less approachable to those who come for our counsel and encouragement.

'Come to me,' said Jesus, and they came. His times communing with the Father may well have remained unseen, yet the depth of that relationship was sensed by a world longing for wisdom, rest and a knowledge of God. And although Jesus was perfect, and we are not, the same can be true of us today.

—— Part 2 ——

FOLLOW ME

*'Follow me… and I will send you
out to fish for people.'*

MATTHEW 4:19

INSPIRATIONAL LEADERSHIP

It started as the idea of Joseph Joffre, the Commander-in-Chief of the French army. It was rapidly accepted by General Sir Douglas Haig, the commander of the British Expeditionary Force. It resulted in more than a million casualties in all, including 58,000 British deaths in just one day—1 July 1916, arguably the darkest day in the history of the British army. And the Battle of the Somme marked the beginning of a new mood in the nation: a new recognition of the futility of war, combined with a growing suspicion of both the wisdom and the motivation of those in authority.

In the context of the events of 1916—and the countless further examples of misleadership, both inept and corrupt, that brought such carnage to the history of the 20th century—it is hardly surprising that a suspicion of authority has been one of the defining features of the past hundred years. In *Truth Is Stranger than It Used to Be*,[1] Richard Middleton and Brian Walsh compare this development to the destruction of the tower of Babel, with the old self-confidence of the modernist tower (founded on science, industry and the market economy) being fatally undermined by the Great War and its attendant horrors—only to be replaced by collapse, confusion, anxiety and a rejection of imperialism in all its forms.

As a philosophy, postmodernism is far more sure of what it stands against than what it stands for. It might best be represented as a large question mark, replacing the confident exclamation mark of its modernist forebears. And one of the clearest targets in the sights of the committed postmodernist is the authoritarian leader who claims to speak (let alone embody) truth. 'Come to me' leadership, accessible leadership, may be culturally acceptable in such a context, but 'Follow me' leadership appears far more problematic.

In reading the Gospels, however, it is impossible to get away from the fact that the command (or invitation), 'Follow me!' played a key role in the leadership style of Jesus. It's not simply that the phrase is famously associated with some of the key moments in his early ministry, as one by one (or two by two) Jesus called fishermen to lay down their nets, zealots to lay down their swords and tax collectors to walk away from their desks. It's not simply that these words found their way into all four Gospels. It is also that the whole theme of 'following Jesus' is intricately woven into the very fabric of the New Testament record, and into the very best of the renewal movements, both monastic and revivalist, that have periodically breathed new integrity and courage into a church that has lost its way.

'Follow me': at first sight the phrase seems out of place in an age increasingly sceptical of authority, but here is where an important distinction needs to be made—between what we say on the one hand and what we do on the other.

Even the most committed of postmodernists recognize the need for leadership in some form (certainly when compared with anarchy, its dreadful alternative). Yet it is leadership integrity, rather than the leadership office, that commands respect today. In terms of the famous phrase from Shakespeare's *Twelfth Night*, there is an equal suspicion of those who are 'born great' and those who 'have greatness thrust upon 'em', but that suspicion does not necessarily extend to those who 'achieve greatness' through lives that match their rhetoric.[2]

There is an irony embedded in this postmodern landscape: at just the point where our value system is at its most confused, we expect our leaders to model a personal integrity of a kind that previous generations would never have demanded. It is no longer possible, for example, for politicians to speak out about the environment without addressing the question of their own carbon footprint—the gas-guzzling car in the garage, the long-distance flights planned for the summer break—nor is it prudent for them to speak on the theme of 'family values' without expecting the most intimate scrutiny of their own domestic credentials. I write this paragraph just 400 metres from Marble Hill House, a large Twickenham mansion built by King George II in the 1720s for his mistress Henrietta Howard. The idea of a member of the royal family being quite so ostentatious about his mistresses today is unthinkable.

In that sense, then, 'Follow me' speaks of an integrity, an authenticity increasingly valued by a world hungry for a leadership that practises what it preaches. 'Follow what I say' may be a debased currency but 'Follow what I do' has retained, even increased, its stock. 'Come to me' leadership, as we have seen, is accessible at its core. 'Follow me' leadership is inspirational. And if we combine the two, bringing together the loving encounter of 'Come to me' with the pioneering adventure of 'Follow me', the result is dynamite.

Private George Morgan took part in the Battle of the Somme on that fateful 1 July and, as one of its survivors, he later wrote this:

There was no lingering when zero hour came. Our platoon officer blew his whistle, and he was the first up the scaling ladder, with his revolver in one hand and a cigarette in the other. 'Come on boys,' he said, and up he went. We went after him one at a time. I never saw the officer again. His name was on the memorial to the missing which they built after the war at Thiepval. He was only young but he was a very brave man.[3]

We might doubt the cause for which that young platoon officer went to his death, but his actions remained inspirational for George Morgan and continue to move us as we read of them today.

There's no exact analogy to Jesus' call to 'Follow me' in the Old Testament, except with regard to God himself. It is true that there's the odd reference to the physical following of a military leader (see, for example, Judges 3:28), and the occasional warning against following a bad role model (for example 2 Kings 14:3). But the word 'follow' in the Old Testament is generally succeeded by the words 'my decrees and laws' or 'justice and justice alone' (Leviticus 18:4; 20:22; Deuteronomy 16:20),[4] while the phrase 'Do not follow' is generally linked with the idolatry and immorality of the nations round about (Leviticus 18:3).

Following God is a feature of some of the Old Testament narratives. Caleb, one of those called by Moses to spy out the promised land, is frequently described by God as someone who 'follows me wholeheartedly' (see Numbers 32:11–12; Deuteronomy 1:36; Joshua 14:8–14), while Elijah famously addresses the crowd on Mount Carmel with the challenge, 'If the Lord is God, follow him!' (1 Kings 18:21). Seldom, though, does an Old Testament narrator call on his readers to follow one of the heroes of faith,[5] and never does one of those heroes dare to say 'Follow me', except in the most literal and prosaic of contexts.

There is a hint of the notion of discipleship in a number of relationships within the Old Testament story, most notably between Moses and Joshua, Eli and Samuel, and Elijah and Elisha. Isaiah seems to have had disciples who memorized his sayings and passed them on to the next generation—'Bind up this testimony of warning', he once said, 'and seal up God's instruction among my disciples' (8:16)—and certainly by the second century BC, Jesus ben Sirach (the author of the book of Ecclesiasticus) could instruct his readers, 'If you discover a wise man, rise early to visit him; let your feet wear out his doorstep' (6:36, NEB).

This concept of discipleship also existed in the Greek culture of the time. Pythagoras, according to Plato, presided over a 'band of intimate disciples who loved him for the inspiration of his society and handed down a way of life which to this day distinguishes the Pythagoreans from the rest of the world'.[6] Socrates (in the words of Xenophon) was 'so useful in all circumstances and in all ways that... the very recollection of him in his absence brought no small good to his constant companions and followers',[7] while Seneca (a contemporary of the apostle Paul) advised his contemporaries to 'choose a master whose life, conversation and soul-expressing face have satisfied you; picture him always to yourself as your protector and pattern.'[8]

In Jesus' day, these influences had fully permeated Jewish culture, with the Gospels themselves referring to the disciples of the Pharisees and the disciples of John (Mark 2:18). Jewish freedom fighters (or terrorists, depending on one's point of view) were surrounded by loyal foot-soldiers—Theudas and Judas the Galilean, for example, who make the briefest of appearances in the Bible during Gamaliel's speech in Acts 5.[9] Rabbis were increasingly developing schools of followers, passing on the faith in a way that was highly practical and related to the most intimate details of daily living. Michael Griffiths draws to our attention one story of a later rabbi, who followed his teacher to the toilet 'to learn how he did it—sitting, not standing, north and south rather than east and west',[10] and while this might seem a rather extreme example, there is something genuinely moving about the quest for personal holiness in the best of the rabbinic writings, and in the conscious modelling of godly behaviour from the rabbi to his disciples.

Jesus was frequently referred to as a rabbi, most often by his disciples themselves,[11] but there's no question that a gulf separated Jesus' practice from that of his contemporaries. For one thing, he called his disciples, rather than allowing them to select him—a practice unparalleled in rabbinic literature and stressed by Jesus himself in those famous words, 'You did not choose me, but I chose you' (John 15:16). For another, the nature of his call was not to a life of study into the intricacies of the Law, with its ultimate goal to turn today's students into tomorrow's teachers. It was rather to a life-changing mission, with its vision to turn disciples, learners, into the most effective missionary force the world has ever seen.

MISLEADERSHIP: BLINDNESS AND HYPOCRISY

One of the saddest stories in the entire Old Testament concerns King David and the appalling series of events that would today be designated 'Bathshebagate'. It's a well-known narrative of sex, violence and the misuse of power, but less well known is the ironic little verse with which the incident is introduced: 'In the spring, at the time when kings go off to war, David sent Joab out with the king's men and the whole Israelite army' (2 Samuel 11:1).

The spring, according to the narrator, is a time 'when kings go off to war'—when kings, in other words, exercise 'Follow me' leadership on the battlefield. That had been David's own style in previous years, from the decisive single-handed victory over the giant Goliath through to further victories over the Philistines, the Amalekites, the Jebusites and all who had stood in Israel's way. Perhaps David was getting a little old for fighting, and the arthritis was starting to set in; and perhaps it was a bit unwise for the king to lead his troops into battle in the first place; and perhaps it was a time for David to exercise 'Go for me' leadership, which, as we will see, is a perfectly legitimate leadership style. But there's something about the juxtaposition of the narrator's opening remarks in 2 Samuel 11 and the sordid events that follow which causes us to reflect on the dangers of misleadership: a misleadership that takes itself out of the front line, proclaiming, in effect, 'Do what I say. Don't do what I do.'

That attitude lay at the heart of Jesus' criticism of the scribes and Pharisees in Matthew 23. It was not simply that their concern for ritual purity rendered them inaccessible and distant in comparison with the accessibility of Jesus' 'Come to me' leadership. It was also that their blindness and hypocrisy highly compromised their ability to act as 'Follow me' leaders. 'The teachers of the law and the Pharisees sit in Moses' seat,' Jesus taught his disciples. 'So you must be careful to do everything they tell you. But do not do what they do, for they do not practise what they preach' (Matthew 23:2–3).

To be fair to the Pharisees, it's unlikely that any of them would have issued the challenge, 'Follow me'. But the sight of religious leaders teaching one thing and living another remained a significant blot on the landscape of the Judaism of Jesus' day; and here it should go without saying that the Church is hardly in a position to cast the first stone.

Physical blindness is, obviously, a medical condition with no sense of fault attached. 'Rabbi, who sinned, this man or his parents, that he was born blind?' asked the disciples in a famous Gospel encounter, to which Jesus responded, 'Neither...' (John 9:2–3). In calling his compatriots 'blind', then (as he does in Matthew 15:14), Jesus was perhaps acknowledging that the culture in which they had been raised had its own blind spots, for which they could not be held ultimately responsible. Yet as the evidence of Jesus' God-given authority grew—as a succession of healings and miracles began to point unequivocally to his messianic calling—so Jesus started to use the words 'blindness' and 'hypocrisy' almost interchangeably. As he put it in John 9:41, 'If you were blind, you would not be guilty of sin; but now that you claim you can see, your guilt remains.'

So what were the features of this blindness and hypocrisy? Some were fairly specific: Luke tells us, for example, that the Pharisees 'loved money' (16:14), a common theme in the Gospel record, against which Jesus directed some of his starkest and most challenging warnings. Mark introduces us to the related concept of 'Corban': a get-out clause that enabled people to dedicate their earnings to God (without paying him a penny!), so circumventing their responsibility to look after their parents (7:11). 'You cannot serve both God and Money,' Jesus stated succinctly in the Sermon on the Mount (Matthew 6:24).

Underlying Jesus' warning not to 'do what they do', however, lay two additional concerns of a more general nature, for the Pharisees' priorities frequently betrayed a lack of perspective on one hand and a lack of integrity on the other.

The first of these—the lack of perspective—was most closely associated with the theme of blindness and expressed itself in the Pharisees' inability to distinguish between the important and the trivial. 'You give a tenth of your spices,' Jesus told them—'mint, dill and cumin. But you have neglected the more important matters of the law—justice, mercy and faithfulness. You should have practised the latter, without neglecting the former. You blind guides! You strain out a gnat but swallow a camel' (Matthew 23:23–24).

As an image, the swallowing of a camel perhaps reminds us of the children's nursery rhyme, 'There was an old woman who swallowed a fly', with its final lines: 'There was an old woman who swallowed a horse. She died, of course.' Yet Jesus' image is more surreal still: our woman is fastidious about the tiny fly in her cup of tea while allowing a camel to barge its way into her mouth and down her throat. How foolish to follow a person with such extraordinary priorities, such a lack of perspective! 'Leave them' says Jesus; 'They are blind guides. If the blind lead the blind, both will fall into a pit' (Matthew 15:14).

The second of Jesus' concerns—the lack of integrity—was most associated with hypocrisy and opened up an alarmingly wide gap between the outer shell and the inner reality. 'You are like white-washed tombs', Jesus described it, 'which look beautiful on the outside but on the inside are full of the bones of the dead and everything unclean' (Matthew 23:27). Under the law, a person who stepped on a grave became ritually unclean (Numbers 19:16), so graves were whitewashed to make them easily visible, especially at night; and this striking image speaks of the heart of hypocrisy—a cultivation of the outward show combined with a total disregard for what is going on inside.

The Greek term for 'hypocrite' literally meant an 'actor'. A hypocrite is someone who acts a role, who plays to the gallery—perhaps (on occasions) a person who enacts the religious part so brilliantly that they convince themselves as much as their audience. Again, says Jesus, such people are not to be followed. Their teaching may be sound enough, so long as they stick to their God-given script, but their love of human applause and their lifestyle when no one is looking makes them quite unsuitable as role models for the would-be disciple.

Os Guinness puts it like this: 'Most of us, whether we are aware of it or not, do things with an eye to the approval of some audience or other. The question is not whether we have an audience but which audience we choose.' And our calling, he continues, is to 'play for an audience of One'.[12]

JESUS THE PIONEER AND PERFECTER

In Hebrews 12:1–2, the author famously writes, 'Therefore, since we are surrounded by such a great cloud of witnesses [the heroes of faith described in chapter 11], let us throw off everything that hinders and the sin that so easily entangles. And let us run with perseverance the race marked out for us, fixing our eyes on Jesus, the pioneer and perfecter of faith.' 'Pioneer and perfecter': neither word is used of Jesus elsewhere in the New Testament, although the Greek root of both words is picked up in the glorious vision of God in Revelation 21:6: 'I am... the Beginning and the End' (v. 6). But while the 'gathering shepherd' is the defining image of 'Come to me' leadership, 'pioneer and perfecter' seems to summarize the essential qualities of the 'Follow me' leader.

Pioneers are, by nature, clear-sighted and courageous. Their mission, like that of the crew of the Starship *Enterprise*, is 'to boldly go where no one has gone before'. There can be a loneliness in pioneering leadership, in the blazing of an unconventional and frequently uncomfortable new trail, yet the best pioneers inspire others to follow, thus becoming far more significant as agents of change than the more conventional (and often more politically powerful) leaders of their day.

'In those days Caesar Augustus issued a decree that a census should be taken of the entire Roman world,' begins Luke 2, and a few verses later we read how a Jewish peasant girl 'gave birth to her firstborn, a son' (v. 7). At that point there seemed no question about the relative significance of Caesar Augustus and the baby placed in a Bethlehem manger. Yet two thousand years later it is Caesar Augustus who plays a cameo role in the story of Jesus of Nazareth, rather than Jesus appearing as a tiny footnote (if at all) in the life of the mighty Caesar.

We have touched on the lack of perspective of many of Jesus' contemporaries who strained out gnats but swallowed camels—an easy critique to make with the benefit of hindsight, though far more difficult when faced with the particular blind spots of our own day. But while blindness (in a purely metaphorical sense) is a characteristic of misleadership, the pioneering leader will frequently view life with an extraordinary clarity that simultaneously inspires some and terrifies others. The Greek term for 'pioneer' in Hebrews 12, *archegos*, carries the sense of an author, a founder, someone bringing us back to the original vision of why we were created. How intriguing that the English word denoting a return to the original foundations of belief—the term 'fundamentalist'—has a similar ability both to inspire and to terrify!

That terror can be justified, of course. It's possible to be both clear-sighted and manipulative, and the deeper the understanding of human beings and human motivation, the greater the danger of that manipulation. And that is where the description of Jesus as the 'perfecter' of our faith perfectly balances his pioneering credentials. A pioneer is exciting to follow but may also be dangerous as a leader. A *perfect* pioneer—someone who both sees clearly and acts with utmost integrity—will be similarly exciting to follow but will also be safe as a leader, not in the sense of offering an easy ride, but safe in the absence of the hypocrisy, manipulation and abuse that have so clouded the record of many a misleader from Jesus' day to our own.

We will shortly focus on the character of Jesus himself as a 'Follow me' leader, but it's interesting first to note the role models that this pioneer and perfecter commended for their right sense of perspective and integrity. A poor widow was praised for her willingness to put 'all she had to live on' into the temple treasury (Mark 12:41–44).[13] A Roman centurion was applauded for the simplicity and directness of his faith (Matthew 8:10). A Samaritan leper was blessed for returning to thank the one who had healed him (Luke 17:16–19). A prostitute was praised for the quality and depth of her love (7:36–50). Destitute widows, Gentiles, Samaritan lepers, prostitutes: none of them would have been an obvious role model in the Israel of Jesus' day, but the reality of their obedience stood in stark contrast to the hypocrisy of those who should have known better.

'Do you see this woman?' asked Jesus of Simon the Pharisee, indicating the prostitute sitting at his feet. 'I came into your house. You did not give me any water for my feet, but she wet my feet with her tears and wiped them with her hair. You did not give me a kiss, but this woman, from the time I entered, has not stopped kissing my feet. You did not put oil on my head, but she has poured perfume on my feet. Therefore, I tell you, her many sins have been forgiven' (Luke 7:44–47).

It's a highly provocative speech on many levels, and a challenge to all religious leaders of a more conventional (or judgmental) hue. Yet it graphically demonstrates an insight that pops up throughout the Bible—that both blindness and hypocrisy on the one hand and clear-sightedness and integrity on the other are frequently to be found in the most unusual places.

Compassion, gentleness, humility, a peaceable spirit, vulnerability: these, as we have seen, are the characteristics of Jesus' 'Come to me' leadership—the accessible, face-to-face encounter that both gathers and embraces. But what of Jesus' 'Follow me' leadership, where all we can see is his back as he strides out into the unknown? The Gospel records point to four further qualities—authority, integrity, insight and self-sacrifice—which help to explain the inspirational nature of Jesus' call for all who are courageous enough to follow.

——— 6 ———

THE CHARACTER OF THE PIONEER AND PERFECTER

AUTHORITY

'Follow me,' said Jesus to his first disciples—and they followed; and the readiness with which they left their homes, their communities and their family businesses is truly remarkable.

That may not be the full story, of course. There is evidence that Jesus knew at least some of the disciples before he issued the call, as John's account seems to suggest (John 1:35–42). But the very words 'Follow me' sounded a note of personal authority that made an immediate and marked impact on the Israel of Jesus' day—a fact well illustrated by Mark's very first editorial comment on the character of Jesus: 'The people were amazed at his teaching, because he taught them as one who had authority, not as the teachers of the law' (1:22).

What, then, was the difference between the ministry of the 'teachers of the law'—a ministry that, as we have seen, was hardly characterized by diffidence or insecurity—and this unique note of authority that so marked the teaching of Jesus?

As we read the Gospels, it becomes clear that both Jesus' claims about himself and the miracles or 'signs' that helped support those claims played a part in establishing him as an authoritative figure, even in those circles where he was increasingly regarded as downright dangerous. One of the first recorded miracles of Jesus, the story of the paralysed man in Mark 2, is a good case in point, where Jesus' claim to be able to forgive a man his sins was combined with a vivid and memorable healing miracle. Whether the miracle proved the claim, or whether Jesus was instead a messenger of Beelzebub, the prince of demons, exercised the minds of his opponents for a while, with most of them eventually plumping for the Beelzebub option, but one fact was indisputable: from the moment Jesus burst on to the Galilean scene, he was most certainly a force to be reckoned with.

Perhaps the heart of the distinction between Jesus' teaching ministry and that of the teachers of the law, though, lay in an area that was a little less tangible than the radical nature of his claims or the power of his miracles. Indeed, the sense of authority that so clearly accompanies some people, and equally clearly eludes others, is often somewhat elusive—a fact that remains deeply frustrating for the hapless teacher whose class is running riot.

In Jesus' case, as we have seen, it was something to do with his ability to see and to live the 'big picture'—to have a pioneer's sense of perspective that consistently focused on the camel rather than the gnat. 'Man shall not live by bread alone,' Jesus famously proclaimed in the wilderness, 'but by every word that comes from the mouth of God' (Matthew 4:4, ESV, quoting Deuteronomy 8:3), and Jesus' ability to feed on God's word, to chew it over, to allow it to become a very part of his being, gave his teaching an extraordinary new perspective. His was the perspective of the 'fundamentalist' (using the word in its very best sense), taking us back to the fundament, the very foundation, of who God is and why we are here.

In English we contrast the 'letter of the law' with the 'spirit of the law'. It's a distinction rooted in the promise of a new covenant made by the Lord through the prophet Jeremiah: 'I will put my law in their minds and write it on their hearts. I will be their God, and they will be my people' (31:33). And as we read, say, the Sermon on the Mount, we recognize the extent to which the law had been written on Jesus' heart, giving him an authority and freedom in its handling that delighted some and shocked others in equal measure.

The scribes were used to proof-texting—quoting passages of the

Law of Moses to back up their point. They would have been happy with Jesus' entirely accurate quotation of the seventh commandment—'You have heard that it was said, "You shall not commit adultery"'—but imagine their surprise and consternation when his very next sentence began with the words, 'But I tell you...' (Matthew 5:27–28). 'Moses said... but I tell you...': who on earth did this jumped-up carpenter think he was?

Of course, Jesus was not contradicting the mighty Moses, although it must have sounded as if he was, but neither was he giving a straightforward commentary on the commandment in the tradition of the scribes and the Pharisees. Instead, Jesus was taking his hearers back to the heart of God's prohibition—to the lust, the sexual addiction, that continues to cause such violence and hatred, oppression and shame today. 'You have heard that it was said... But I tell you that anyone who looks at a woman lustfully has already committed adultery with her in his heart.'

When we speak of the 'spirit of the law', it tends to be with a view to lessening its demands upon us: 'Yes, I *was* travelling at 40 mph in a 30 mph area, but I did keep a close lookout for pedestrians, so it was very much in the spirit of the law.' But the challenging nature of the Sermon on the Mount lies in its unsettling insight that the spirit of the law can sometimes be tougher than the letter of the law. Indeed, Jesus spelt out that insight in unequivocal terms: 'I tell you that unless your righteousness surpasses that of the Pharisees and the teachers of the law, you will certainly not enter the kingdom of heaven' (Matthew 5:20).

Yet the same Jesus who plumbed the depths of the heart of the law of God equally plumbed the depths of the love of God. In John 8, we read how a woman was brought before him who had plainly broken the seventh commandment (though it takes two to tango, and her accomplice was strangely missing from the scene). The law of God was duly invoked, by which she should have been stoned to death. And as he quietly drew in the sand, perhaps Jesus was thinking of the purpose of God's law—its potential to lead men and women to repentance, as in the great revivals of the past under Solomon and Hezekiah, Josiah and the Maccabees.

The sight of the men standing round, stones in hand, using the woman as a bait with which to trap Jesus—playing with her life as a way of catching a bigger fish—was far removed from that godly purpose. So Jesus unerringly pointed not to the woman but to her accusers: 'Let any one of you who is without sin be the first to throw a stone at her' (v. 7); and only when they had gone did he face the woman herself, expressing both forgiveness and a clear but gentle call to repentance. The depth of human sin; the depth of God's grace! As some took offence at Jesus' teaching and 'no longer followed him', it's hardly surprising that others—led by the irrepressible Simon Peter—were forced to conclude, 'Lord, to whom shall we go? You have the words of eternal life' (John 6:66, 68).

I've always liked the phrase 'Petty Officer'. It is the naval equivalent of a sergeant in the army, and is the lowest of the senior rating grades. And I'm sure Petty Officers have their place in the Navy, but in the world outside, a literal petty officer—one who spends his or her life patrolling the boundaries of the trivial—will never make a 'Follow me' leader, as the example of the scribes and Pharisees so vividly demonstrates.

'Follow me,' said Jesus, and people followed, because here was a man whose perspective went further and wider and deeper than anyone else's. 'The people were amazed at his teaching, because he taught them as one who had authority, not as the teachers of the law' (Mark 1:22).

INTEGRITY

Seeing the big picture is one thing, but living it is quite another, and there is no question that personal integrity was a second key aspect of Jesus' 'Follow me' magnetism. He was a 'lamb without blemish or defect', as we read in Peter's first letter: 'he committed no sin, and no deceit was found in his mouth' (1:19; 2:22).[1] 'In him is no sin,' concurs John (1 John 3:5)—and that despite his previous assertion that 'if we claim to be without sin we deceive ourselves and the truth is not in us' (1:8). He is 'holy, blameless, pure, set apart from sinners, exalted above the heavens' according to the writer to the Hebrews (7:26), while Paul too assumes the complete innocence of Christ in an explanation of the cross which is as pithy as it is profound: 'God made him who had no sin to be sin for us, so that in him we might become the righteousness of God' (2 Corinthians 5:21).

The word 'integrity' is derived from the Latin *integer*, meaning 'whole' or 'complete', and that wholeness, that sense of a completely integrated personality, makes the New Testament's portrait of Jesus highly rounded and hugely attractive. Disintegrity leads to a disintegration between the outer and the inner, between one part of our lives and another, between word and deed. 'Do everything they tell you… but do not do what they do' is a classic pointer to such disintegration in the life of the misleader. But with Jesus there was no sense of a mismatch between who he was and who he presented himself to be—no distinction between what he taught and how he lived. Yes, his opponents could accuse him of troublemaking or sabbath breaking or gluttony, but no one either could or did pin him with the charge of hypocrisy.

It would be pointless to go through the Gospels picking out examples of Jesus' integrity, for this quality underlies the entire record of a man 'full of grace and truth' (John 1:14). Luke gives us a snapshot of an early trip to Jerusalem, in which Jesus astonished the temple authorities with his precocious insight and understanding. 'As Jesus grew up', that story concludes, 'he increased in wisdom and in favour with God and people' (2:52). All four Gospel writers give us many further insights into Jesus' ability to 'walk the walk' as well as 'talk the talk', somehow holding together grace and truth in the most glorious and (frequently) unpredictable of ways. Even at the end, at his weakest and most vulnerable, Jesus' integrity shone out, as the 'seven words from the cross' so graphically demonstrate. 'When the centurion, who stood there in front of Jesus, saw how he died,' Mark writes, 'he said, "Surely this man was the Son of God!"' (15:39).

It's easy to take such accounts for granted, especially for those whose reading of the Gospels has become dulled by over-familiarity, but the reality is that it's extremely difficult to portray true goodness in a way that doesn't drift into hard-edged judgmentalism or gooey sentimentality. In his *Preface to Paradise Lost*, C.S. Lewis sought to respond to an observation frequently made by readers of the epic poem—that Satan is by far the most interesting of Milton's characters. 'The reason,' he wrote, 'is not hard to find':

Set a hundred poets to tell the same story and in ninety of the resulting poems Satan will be the best character… To make a character worse than oneself it is only necessary to release imaginatively from control some of the bad passions which, in real life, are always straining at the leash… But if you try to draw a character better than yourself, all you can do is to take the best moments you have had and to imagine them prolonged and more consistently embodied in action. The real high virtues which we do not possess at all, we cannot depict except in a purely external fashion. We do not really know what it feels like to be a man [sic] much better than ourselves. His whole inner landscape is one we have never seen, and when we guess it we blunder… Heaven understands Hell and Hell does not understand Heaven.[2]

In such a context, the portrait of Jesus' integrity that emerges from the Gospel pages without any such guesses or blunders is so vivid, so compelling as to point in one of two directions: either to the most extraordinary of storytellers or (as is rather the case) to the most extraordinary of subjects around whom the story revolves.

INSIGHT

'Follow me,' said Jesus, 'and I will send you out to fish for people' (Matthew 4:19). In other words, 'Follow me because I can teach you something. I can show you how to use the gift you have—the ability to fish—in a way that will reap a significant, even eternal, harvest.' And at once they left their nets and followed him.

Here is a third character trait that the 'Follow me' leader needs to develop: not simply the ability both to grasp and live the big picture of what life's about and why we're here, but also the insight to help individuals relate their own experiences to that big picture and recognize their significance within it.[3] If someone can show us how to make the most of our time here on earth, if someone can demonstrate how our lives in all their ordinariness can have an extraordinary impact, if someone can recognize the gifts within us and help us develop those gifts to their fullest potential, then we will follow that person to the ends of the earth.

There's a theme that plays out in much popular literature, especially books written for children—the theme of unimportant people in one world discovering themselves to be highly important in another. Whether it's Charlie who discovers his worth in the deliciously dangerous environment of Willy Wonka's chocolate factory, four child evacuees who find that they are kings and queens in the land of Narnia, or Frodo Baggins, a humble hobbit on whose narrow shoulders the future of Tolkien's universe seems to rest,[4] the popularity of the books based around this theme suggests that it connects with a key need in the human psyche—the need for a sense of personal significance.

And as we read the 'Follow me' passages in the Gospels, it becomes clear that Jesus both recognizes this need and responds to it. 'Simon' (literally 'one who listens') is called Peter (the rock): 'and on this rock I will build my church' (Matthew 16:18). Simon and Andrew, James and John—four fishers of fish—are called instead to be kingdom fishers, fishers of people. 'When the Son of Man sits on his glorious throne', says Jesus to the apostles, 'you who have followed me will also sit on twelve thrones, judging the twelve tribes of Israel. And everyone who has left houses or brothers or sisters or father or mother or children or fields for my sake will receive a hundred times as much and will inherit eternal life' (Matthew 19:28–29).

In the wrong hands, such leadership insight could be horribly misused. Many manipulative misleaders have used flattery and the promise of significance to achieve their selfish and frequently ugly ends, but for Jesus there was complete integrity in his 'Follow me' call. For one thing, he entirely (and remarkably) believed in the potential of those whom he was calling; for another, he was wholly willing to invest great resources of time and energy to see that potential become a reality.

At the heart of the matter—and at the intersection of the 'Come to me' and 'Follow me' approaches to leadership—lies the question of relationship. Any attempt to bypass the building of good, trusting relationships will seriously compromise the leader's ability to lead, however sound their strategies and strong their communication skills.[5] The good shepherd, says Jesus, 'calls his own sheep by name and leads them out'. The sheep 'follow him because they know his voice', and this relationship of mutual love and trust is founded on the shepherd's clear commitment to the well-being and growth of the flock: 'The thief comes only to steal and kill and destroy; I have come that they may have life, and have it to the full' (John 10:3, 4, 10).

Whatever the strength (or otherwise) of their pastoral abilities, 'Follow me' leaders need to recognize a basic truth: their job is not simply to get their job done. It is rather to get their job done while developing others to do it as well as or better than they do it themselves.[6] We might enjoy leading an organization; we might thrive under the weight of considerable responsibilities; but if we're doing it on our own, without seeking to develop other leaders, then whatever gifts we have will die with us. And as Jesus' own priorities demonstrate, there can be no success without a successor—or, better still, a dozen successors trained to continue the work in the generations to come.[7]

SELF-SACRIFICE

A final, most challenging, character trait implied in the phrase 'Follow me' is that of self-sacrifice, of courage, of a willingness to embrace the suffering that is always implicit in the call of the pioneer. Peter writes, 'To this you were called, because Christ suffered for you, leaving you an example, that you should follow in his steps' (1 Peter 2:21).

In Matthew's Gospel, an enthusiastic teacher of the law came to Jesus and exclaimed, 'Teacher, I will follow you wherever you go.' 'Foxes have holes and birds have nests, but the Son of Man has nowhere to lay his head,' was Jesus' somewhat sobering response (8:19–20). A little later in the same Gospel, Peter tried to dissuade Jesus from embracing his call to suffer and die. 'Whoever wants to be my disciple must deny themselves and take up their cross and follow me,' replied Jesus (16:24). Three chapters on, a rich young man came to Jesus and asked, 'Teacher, what good thing must I do to get eternal life?' 'Go, sell your possessions and give to the poor,' said Jesus, 'and you will have treasure in heaven. Then come, follow me' (19:16, 21).

What gives these passages their bite is the fact that Jesus wasn't asking anyone to do something he was unwilling to do himself. Indeed, that, by definition, is the essence of 'Follow me' leadership. 'I am homeless,' says Jesus—'less comfortable than a fox or a bird— so if you follow me, you will be uncomfortable too. I'm on my way to crucifixion, so if you follow me you will need to take up your cross as well. I don't have any possessions, so hold lightly to yours if you want to follow me. I'm washing your feet, so you must wash one another's feet' (see John 13:14).

Mark 8 is an intriguing chapter, which further develops this theme. In verse 22 we are introduced to a blind man from Bethsaida. Jesus prays for his healing and, for the only time in the Gospels, the healing is at first incomplete. 'I see people', says the man; 'they look like trees walking around' (v. 24). Once again Jesus lays hands on the man, and this time his eyes are opened, his sight is restored and he can see everything perfectly.

Immediately afterwards, we read of Simon Peter's confession at Caesarea Philippi. 'You are the Messiah!' he proclaims, his eyes miraculously opened to the true identity of his Master. Like the blind man, though, his vision is still incomplete. '[Jesus] then began to teach them that the Son of Man must suffer many things and be rejected by the elders, the chief priests and the teachers of the law, and that he must be killed and after three days rise again. He spoke plainly about this, and Peter took him aside and began to rebuke him' (vv. 29, 31–32).

'Get behind me, Satan' was Jesus' tough response to his partially sighted disciple, as he recognized in Peter's words the same temptations that had so battered him during his 40 days in the wilderness: 'You do not have in mind the concerns of God, but merely human concerns' (v. 33). And while Jesus' mission to give up his life for us was clearly unique, the New Testament is equally clear that the notion of self-sacrifice can never be detached from the 'Follow me' call to discipleship.

Jesus told a challenging little parable in Matthew 13:44: the story of some treasure that a man found in a field.[8] In his joy, the man sold all he had to buy the field and claim the treasure as his own. The power of the parable lies simply in this—that the man who was telling the story was also the man who wholly embodied it. Jesus joyfully invested everything in the kingdom of heaven. No wonder he was disappointed at others who proved unwilling to do the same.[9]

In a previous chapter we saw how Jesus' access to the Father lay at the heart of his ability as a 'Come to me' leader. As we look at his 'Follow me' qualities—the authority, integrity, insight and self-sacrifice that so inspired many of his contemporaries—the core value linking all of these attributes can be summarized in the phrase 'obedience to the Father'. Jesus had authority because he was under authority, and this forms the theme of the following chapter.

✥

———— 7 ————

JESUS' OBEDIENCE TO THE FATHER

Jesus was not often taken by surprise. Yet the case of the Roman centurion who came to him with a pressing need in Matthew 8:5–13 was a notable exception. The centurion's servant was seriously ill at home and, despite Jesus' willingness to come and heal him, the centurion unexpectedly turned down the offer. 'Lord, I do not deserve to have you come under my roof,' he replied. 'But just say the word, and my servant will be healed. For I myself am a man under authority, with soldiers under me. I tell this one, "Go," and he goes; and that one, "Come," and he comes' (vv. 8–9). 'I have not found anyone in Israel with such great faith,' responded Jesus in genuine astonishment (v. 10)—and the servant was duly healed.

It's an fascinating passage, not least because of the links that the centurion makes between his own experience and that of Jesus. In one sense, the soldier acknowledged the huge gulf that separated the two of them: his words 'I do not deserve to have you come under my roof' come across as entirely genuine, impressively so given the relative status that society must have granted to their contrasting callings. In another sense, though the man recognized some intriguing parallels.

Commentators have often emphasized one of those parallels—that both the centurion and Jesus exercised authority (over men in one case and sickness in another)—but, interestingly, that's not where the centurion began. 'I myself am a man *under* authority' was his starting point, for it was on that basis that he (and, by implication, Jesus) exercised the authority entrusted to him. It's true that Jesus the Son of God had an authority that the centurion could only dream about, 'far above all rule and authority, power and dominion, and every name that can be invoked, not only in the present age but also in the one to come' (Ephesians 1:21). But even then, this meeting essentially took place between two men who knew what it was to live under authority. Perhaps that is why the centurion felt safe enough to approach Jesus in the first place.

Jesus' own sense of being a man under authority has already been mentioned in the Introduction, in terms of those telling phrases from John's Gospel: 'My food is to do the will of him who sent me and to finish his work' (4:34); 'The Son can do nothing by himself; he can do only what he sees his Father doing' (5:19); 'What I have heard from him I tell the world... I always do what pleases him' (8:26, 29); 'I did not speak on my own, but the Father who sent me commanded me to say all that I have spoken' (12:49). If the misleadership of Jesus' day was characterized by blindness and hypocrisy, these verses speak instead of a complete surefootedness, both in Jesus' understanding of what he was meant to be doing and in his willingness to get on and do it.

The various accounts of Jesus' baptism and temptations flesh out this theme further, demonstrating both his understanding and his obedience in a nutshell. Jesus was baptized and, as he emerged from the water, he saw the Spirit descending on him like a dove, and heard the word of God spoken over him: 'You are my Son, whom I love; with you I am well pleased' (Mark 1:11). Immediately afterwards the Spirit drove him out into the desert, and there he was tested for 40 days, during which time (according to Matthew 4 and Luke 4) he placed himself firmly under the authority of the written word of God, rebutting the devil's insidious temptations with the persistent phrase, 'It is written'.[1] At the end of this highly demanding experience, Jesus was strengthened by fresh encouragement from his Father in the form of angels who 'came and attended him' (Matthew 4:11), before being launched into the public arena.

Such accounts make disturbing reading for those who look to the word of God for comfort and to the Spirit of God for a sense of warmth, peace and personal well-being. It's true that Jesus received the affirmation of the Father at the beginning of the story (and it is significant that the Father was 'well pleased' with his Son even before Jesus had begun his ministry of teaching and healing). It is also true that Jesus received the encouragement of angels at the end. But the picture of the Spirit 'driving' him into the desert (Mark 1:12, ESV—the same word that is used of the driving out of the money changers in John 2) and the use of the phrase 'It is written' to keep Jesus walking along the costly path of discipleship act as necessary reminders of the uncomfortable challenge of taking up our cross and following him.

These accounts stress, too, the importance of both word and Spirit: Jesus was equally attuned to the scriptures and to the guiding presence of God himself. The Pharisees may have known their scriptures but they seemed deaf to the voice of the Spirit;[2] the Sadducees, worse still, did not know the scriptures or the power of God (Matthew 22:29). But for Jesus, his dual commitment to word and Spirit gave him both a rootedness and a freedom that made (and make) the path of discipleship a godly adventure, a journey of faith.

Was Jesus calling his disciples to be conservatives or radicals along that path? It's an intriguing question. Perhaps, to borrow an image from John Stott, he was calling them to resemble neither the caged bird of the fundamentalist[3] (with a capacity for flight but no freedom to use it), nor the free-floating balloon of the radical (buoyant, unrestrained, with no anchorage and no accountability except to itself); but rather to be like a kite, which can 'take off, fly great distances and soar to great heights, while all the time being tethered to earth'.[4] Rootedness and freedom: Jesus knew them both in his obedience to the Father, and expected them both in those who came after him. 'If you love me, keep my commands' (John 14:15), he could say in one breath and, in another, 'The wind blows wherever it pleases... So it is with everyone born of the Spirit' (3:8).

The story of the exodus once again provides us (and provided Jesus) with inspiration at this point. For alongside the tent of meeting, the place where 'the Lord would speak to Moses face to face, as one speaks to a friend' (Exodus 33:11), the narrative introduces us to further images of tablets of stone and pillars of cloud and fire.

The tablets of stone symbolize Moses' great role as the law giver (or, perhaps more accurately, law mediator) to Israel—his commitment under God to promote order, justice, holiness and cohesion among God's people through the Ten Commandments and the many lesser decrees and regulations scattered throughout the Pentateuch. Whatever the later discussions concerning the role and purpose of the law, and whatever the precise meaning of Jesus' famous statement, 'Do not think that I have come to abolish the Law or the Prophets; I have not come to abolish them but to fulfil them' (Matthew 5:17), there was never any question of the need for rootedness in the Judeo-Christian tradition. We need an objective morality to provide the boundaries of the pitch on which the game of life is played.

The pillars of cloud and fire remind us of Moses' related role as a prophet, called to recognize and follow the presence of God. Alongside the undoubted need for an objective morality, there was a parallel need for guidance on a daily basis—for a sense of direction and purpose, to set right priorities in the midst of the messiness and perplexity of daily living. So we read, 'By day the Lord went ahead of them in a pillar of cloud to guide them on their way and by night in a pillar of fire to give them light, so that they could travel by day or night' (Exodus 13:21).

Both cloud and fire are symbols of the Lord's presence, a presence that simultaneously evokes comfort, strength, guidance, awe, mystery and fear. In an illuminating passage in Exodus 33, we find Moses approaching the Lord with the request, 'If you are pleased with me, teach me your ways so I may know you and continue to find favour with you' (v. 13). The Lord, rather than giving Moses another law book to digest, replies, 'My Presence will go with you, and I will give you rest.' 'If your Presence does not go with us, do not send us up from here,' continues Moses. 'What else will distinguish me and your people from all the other people on the face of the earth?' (vv. 14–16). Moses knew—and so did the Lord— that the law was not enough to set Israel apart from the other nations. First and foremost, Israel was called to be a people of the presence of God.

Right from the beginning of Israel's history as a holy nation, then, the idea of word and Spirit, tablets and pillars, law and presence, rules and relationship, was built into the nation's understanding of what it meant to be a holy people. Obedience was not simply a question of filling in a legalistic questionnaire and ticking all the right boxes. It was also a question of following the promptings of God, being led by his presence, keeping in step with the Spirit.

When Jesus was summoned to the house of Jairus with the urgent request to heal his terminally ill daughter—and when, on the way, a sick woman touched the edge of his cloak and was instantly healed—there was nothing in the law to tell Jesus exactly what to do next: whether to attend to the twelve-year-old girl or the older woman's twelve-year-old ailment. That is one of the limitations of the law: it cannot, in itself, guide us to choose either the lesser of two evils or the greater of two goods. It was only through keeping in step with the Spirit that Jesus could choose to give the woman some time and attention—culminating in those encouraging words, 'Daughter, your faith has healed you. Go in peace and be freed from your suffering'—before attending to the synagogue owner's daughter and raising her from the dead (Mark 5:21–43).

This is an extraordinary approach to daily living, we might think. It suggests a degree of spontaneity and flexibility that makes the average time management guru look pedestrian and flatfooted by comparison. But the rooted freedom that we witness in the Jesus of the Gospels remains a constant challenge to both the caged fundamentalists and the free-floating radicals of every generation. Pure dependence on the scriptures is not enough. Pure dependence on the Spirit of God is not enough. For we are fallible creatures and even a wholehearted commitment to be blown by the wind of the Spirit can all too easily drift into a growing acceptance of the spirit of the age, in the natural but wholly misguided quest for a faith that causes no offence—that conveniently fits me and condones my chosen lifestyle.

Jesus' obedience during his 40 days in the wilderness was, in a sense, a dress rehearsal for the events of Holy Week, just as David's private battles against lions and bears equipped him for the duel with Goliath in 1 Samuel 17. The ancient hymn recorded for us in Philippians 2 reminds us of the downward mobility of a man who 'being in very nature God... made himself nothing... becoming obedient to death—even death on a cross' (vv. 6–8). The writer to the Hebrews speaks of how Jesus 'learned obedience from what he suffered' (5:8)—learning day by day to place his will beneath the will of his Father. This was what gave Jesus his authority—his ability to focus on the big picture as he meditated on the scriptures and opened himself to the empowering of the Spirit. This lay at the heart of his integrity, his insight and his acceptance of a ministry that had self-sacrifice at its very core.

And this is what makes Jesus the ultimate 'Follow me' leader, whose character and calling have continued to inspire and motivate some of the most remarkable men and women of the past two millennia.

✣

--------- 8 ---------

WALKING THE WAY OF COSTLY GRACE

Wednesday 12 June: Thus far [I wrote in my diary] *we have behaved like model Western tourists, of the kind that officials at the communist China International Travel Service dream of. But this evening we made our first foray away from the tourist circuit, and went to visit Pastor M and his wife in their home.*

Pastor M is one of maybe five living men who endured appalling persecution under Mao and who are regarded with considerable reverence in Chinese house-church circles: 'bishops' in the line of Polycarp and Ignatius of Antioch. Imprisoned for 24 years from 1955 to 1979, M was constantly manacled and shackled, with a daily regime of hard labour and re-education classes. 'Do you love God? Do you love Jesus?' his tormentors would ask him, questions followed by a sharp tug at the ropes that covered his emaciated body. During this time he was largely isolated from other Christians, and kept alive by the Bible verses and hymns that he'd learnt from childhood. 'It was at the most unexpected moments that God gave me strength, even joy,' he told me, as we reflected on the almost unimaginable suffering this man had endured.

Commenting on the current persecution endured by unofficial house churches today, Pastor M acknowledged that things weren't too bad (in comparative terms) especially in the cities; but went on to speak of the widespread system of prison sentences and fines imposed on churches and Christians for not registering with the government—a particularly difficult situation in poorer country areas. One church had had their pastor imprisoned, and was asked to find 50,000 yuan (nearly £5000) to have him released: a huge sum, far beyond the capabilities of a typical rural congregation. Others—in the wake of the crackdown following the Falun Gong demonstrations—had had their church buildings bulldozed.

Pastor M knew of at least 2000 house churches meeting in the Beijing area, with growing evangelism among both the poor and the intellectuals. Many of these churches were predominantly young, and most numbered fewer than 100 members. M himself visited many such Churches each year, to train and ordain leaders, and to baptize hundreds of converts. His biggest concern was the paucity of mature leaders in their 50s and 60s, to whom he could pass on the baton of spiritual oversight, and the consequent development of splinter groups and some distinctly unusual cults.

Following a prayer and a hymn, we made our way downstairs for dinner. Outside the security of his flat, M and his wife both seemed fairly wary and on their guard. But we found a quiet corner of the restaurant to continue our conversation.

The self-sacrificial obedience that lies at the heart of 'Follow me' leadership is daily lived out in the ministry of those like Pastor M, whom I was privileged to meet during an inspiring trip to China in 2002.

During that month in China, I committed myself to reading the New Testament in the light of what I was experiencing, and to writing down every reference I could find to hardship, persecution, misunderstanding and self-sacrifice. Had I taken a pair of scissors and cut those references out, the whole book would have fallen apart. For the truth is that Jesus expected his followers to undergo the kind of sufferings that Pastor M endured: they are not (as we sometimes imagine from a comfortable Western perspective) the eccentric experience of a few believers who have the misfortune to be born in the wrong place at the wrong time.

The apostle Paul provides a clear example in this regard, for his encounter with the risen Christ on the Damascus road, and his subsequent decision to leave behind his privileged background and become a 'fool for Christ', made hardship a regular theme across his writings.

Comparing himself to the so-called 'super-apostles' in 2 Corinthians 11, Paul felt prompted to write of his weaknesses and sufferings. He writes:

I have worked much harder [than them], been in prison more frequently, been flogged more severely, and been exposed to death again and again. Five times I received... the forty lashes minus one. Three times I was beaten with rods, once I was pelted with stones, three times I was ship-wrecked, I spent a night and a day in the open sea, I have been constantly on the move... Besides everything else, I face daily the pressure of my concern for all the churches. Who is weak, and I do not feel weak? Who is led into sin, and I do not inwardly burn? (vv. 23–26, 28–29)

In his correspondence with the Thessalonians, too, Paul could write of himself as a role model, a 'Follow me' leader, in this regard:

You yourselves know how you ought to follow our example. We were not idle when we were with you, nor did we eat anyone's food without paying for it. On the contrary, we worked night and day, labouring and toiling so that we would not be a burden to any of you. We did this, not because we do not have the right to such help, but in order to offer ourselves as a model for you to imitate. (2 Thessalonians 3:7–9)

'Join with me in suffering, like a good soldier of Christ Jesus,' he concludes to the young leader Timothy, and stresses, 'Everyone who wants to live a godly life in Christ Jesus will be persecuted' (2 Timothy 2:3; 3:12). And it was probably in the early 60s AD and by personal instruction of the Emperor Nero that Paul paid the ultimate cost of discipleship with his life.

WHAT'S SO AMAZING ABOUT OBEDIENCE?

What's So Amazing about Grace? is the name of a bestselling book written by Philip Yancey.[1] The heart of Yancey's teaching focuses around the memorable phrases, 'There is nothing we can do to make God love us more. There is nothing we can do to make God love us less', and these truths are developed during the course of the book, with good exegesis and some moving illustrations and stories.

Yet, as a summary of the Christian venture as a whole, Yancey's phrases remain one-sided, even (in the wrong hands) seriously misleading. For the reality of Jesus' 'Follow me' teaching and the lifestyle that embodies it suggest that obedience, alongside grace, is a critical part of the gospel package—that Christians are called to a life of repentance, costly integrity and growing sanctification through daily obedience to the word and Spirit of God. Unconditional love is indeed a wonderful characteristic of the God and Father of our Lord Jesus Christ, but the Bible is also crammed full of conditional clauses as to God's blessings—a fact that a somewhat laborious Bible study on the little word 'if' would clearly demonstrate.

Alongside Yancey's book, then, we need to hold the insights of Dietrich Bonhoeffer's *The Cost of Discipleship*,[2] with his timely warnings of the dangers of cheap grace. 'Cheap grace,' the book begins arrestingly, 'is the deadly enemy of our Church. We are fighting today for costly grace.' It continues:

Cheap grace is the preaching of forgiveness without requiring repentance, baptism without church discipline, communion without confession... Cheap grace is grace without discipleship, grace without the cross, grace without Jesus Christ, living and incarnate.

This cheap grace has been... disastrous to our own spiritual lives. Instead of opening up the way to Christ it has closed it. Instead of calling us to follow Christ, it has hardened us in our disobedience.

They are stirring words, made all the more powerful by the context in which they were written. Bonhoeffer's own commitment to 'costly grace' was soon put to the test as he faced imprisonment, then death, at the hands of the Nazi authorities. Despite its historical specificity, however, no one looking at today's church (especially the church in the West) could reasonably ignore the continuing relevance of Bonhoeffer's challenge. For the irony is that those parts of the world where Christians already have it comparatively easy—where there is very little by way of persecution or hardship—tend to be the very areas where the church is in most danger of watering down the faith still further.

The call to a simple lifestyle in the face of world poverty and environmental catastrophe, the call to sexual abstinence for those not blessed with the gift of marriage, the call to marital fidelity for those who are: these can all too easily become the latest victims in the rise of cheap grace, seducing us to the 'mediocre level of the world' and 'quenching the joy of discipleship', to use Bonhoeffer's words once more.[3]

Even one of the great sacred cows of our age—the much-heralded 'work-life balance'—should perhaps be placed under the Bonhoeffer spotlight. Today's constant quest to achieve the most balanced of lifestyles, however well-intentioned, can all too easily become a cover for self-indulgence, so blunting the cutting edge of Jesus' call. 'Surely you remember, brothers and sisters, our toil and hardship,' wrote Paul in 1 Thessalonians 2:9; 'we worked night and day in order not to be a burden to anyone', and while this teaching, undiluted, could lead to pastoral burnout, it is vitally important not to let the pendulum swing too far the other way.

There's the danger of a false dichotomy at this point, of course. It is important that both leaders and followers take proper time to rest and that they're free to enjoy the much-trumpeted 'quality time' with their families and friends. But achieving a balanced life is in itself too feeble an ambition, too comfortable, too lacking in passion and adventure for the 'Follow me' leader to settle for. 'Ask hungry children in Somalia if they want to help you achieve balance,' writes John Ortberg, 'and you'll quickly find that they were hoping for something more from you.'[4]

'Follow me' leadership, in other words, is about achieving

godliness more than achieving balance—seeking first the kingdom of God and his righteousness (Matthew 6:33), rather than making a stressfree existence our ultimate aim.

Both blindness and hypocrisy lay at the heart of the mis-leadership of some of Jesus' contemporaries and rendered them useless, even harmful, as 'Follow me' leaders. The combination of a lack of perspective and a lack of integrity opened the way for a faith that was narrow and blinkered on the one hand, and dishonest and disillusioning on the other.

Hypocrisy is perhaps the easier of the leadership sins both to recognize and to pass judgment on. I know of a local church that is pulling itself apart over the extramarital affair of its senior pastor, and the result of such misleadership is clear to see in the dispirited faces of its members.

Yet blindness—a lack of perspective—may have less obvious ramifications in the life of a Christian leader but can still do untold damage to the Church of Christ. Scholars tell us that the famous translation of Proverbs 29:18 in the Authorized Version is not especially accurate: 'Where there is no vision, the people perish'. Although they're right, this verse must qualify as one of the most inspired mistranslations of all time!

What does visionless leadership look like? The preaching may focus on the minutiae of human behaviour, while neglecting the 'more important matters of the law—justice, mercy and faithful-ness' (Matthew 23:23). The leadership may be endlessly responding to 101 little demands on its time, without standing back to see the big picture. It may be a perfectionist leadership, obsessed with the perfect rendition of a choral setting or the micro-management of a flawless worship session, to the exclusion of almost anything else. It may be a leadership so small in vision that Simon the fisherman remains Simon the fisherman, with his Peter-potential wholly un-tapped. Such leadership can be hardworking (impressively so, on occasions) while achieving very little, presiding over a fellowship that becomes increasingly narrowminded, ineffective and feeble.

The tabloid press takes great pleasure in exposing hypocrisy—often doing so in the most hypocritical way possible, juxtaposing the 'naughty vicar' story on page 2 with the naked model on page 3. Perhaps, though, blindness is in reality the greater enemy of the Church. When obedience is reduced to ticking boxes on a moral or liturgical questionnaire, and where the Spirit, who 'blows where he wills', is increasingly cold-shouldered by a leadership intent on following its own agenda, then the cage of the fundamentalist beckons and the free-but-anchored kite is quietly put away in its box. It's no wonder (to change the image) that some churches try quite so hard to pour the new wine of the gospel of Jesus Christ into the old wineskins of pharisaic legalism, despite Jesus' warnings of the impossibility of such an exercise (Matthew 9:17).

Where, then, do we learn the obedience that lies at the heart of 'Follow me' leadership? How do we grow in the qualities of authority, integrity, insight and self-sacrifice? We do so, I suggest, by attending to the tablets and the pillars, the word and the Spirit of God.

TABLETS AND PILLARS

In 2 Timothy 3:15, Paul writes to his protégé Timothy of 'how from infancy you have known the Holy Scriptures, which are able to make you wise for salvation through faith in Christ Jesus'—and, by the grace of God, the same could be said of me. When I was very young, my grandmother used to send me Bible reading notes from her house in the Chilterns—notes produced by the Bible Reading Fellowship (which seems somewhat appropriate since that is the excellent organization which has agreed to publish this book!) And despite my wandering attention span and a varying degree of commitment to the enterprise, I am eternally grateful for the early love of the scriptures that my grandmother's thoughtfulness instilled in me.

The scriptures contain much that is (in the warmest sense of the word) 'comfortable'. 'Hear what comfortable words our Saviour Christ saith unto all that truly turn to him,' the old Prayer Book says, followed by the greatest 'Come to me' of them all: 'Come unto me all that travail and are heavy laden, and I will refresh you.'[5] But the scriptures also contain many challenges, some of the sharpest of which are found on the lips of Jesus himself—challenges that cut right across our usual ethical distinctions between social justice and personal morality, and therefore pose a problem for all who would dare to create a god in their own image, whether a left-wing or a right-wing variety. 'It ain't the parts of the Bible that I can't understand that bother me,' Mark Twain once famously remarked: 'it's the parts that I do understand'; and there's something about attending to the challenge of scripture—meditating on the bothering bits that we *do* understand—which seems, to me, key to living a life of genuine Christian integrity.

This is not to suggest that the Bible is always easy to understand or that biblical scholarship (a genuine teasing-out of the context and meaning of the scriptures) is anything other than a thoroughly honourable occupation. But wherever attempts to understand the Bible begin to resemble efforts to undermine the Bible, wherever Christians choose to judge scripture rather than coming beneath its authority, and wherever we opt too quickly for approaches to the text that leave our lifestyle unchallenged and our composure un-ruffled, there is almost certainly something wrong. Even those who are profoundly committed to the authority of scripture can all too easily develop major blind spots in this regard. It was, after all, the Pharisees and the Sadducees—those guardians of the tablets and the temple—who conspired to put Jesus to death.

How, then, in our commitment to understand and obey the scriptures, do we avoid a kind of neo-legalism in our own lives and the lives of those we lead? How do we root our lives in the scriptures, as Jesus did, without sacrificing freedom of movement? Here's where the insight of Exodus 33 really helps. As Christians, it is true that we have a far fuller revelation of God's character and purposes than Moses ever had. With the entire Old Testament to guide us and, more significantly still, the New Testament with its glorious portrayal of Jesus the Word-made-flesh, we might be thought to have everything we need for authentic Christian living. Yet Moses' request still stands: 'If you are pleased with me, teach me your ways so I may know you and continue to find favour with you'. The Lord's response, too, is still of the utmost relevance: 'My Presence will go with you, and I will give you rest' (Exodus 33:13–14).

We need the pillars as well as the tablets—the Spirit alongside the word of God—for 'where the Spirit of the Lord is, there is freedom' (2 Corinthians 3:17).

As the leader of a large church in the evangelical-charismatic tradition, I must confess to being a somewhat reluctant charismatic at times. I have seen quite enough evidence of the love and power of God's Spirit—occasionally in the most extraordinary, inspiring and miraculous of ways—to overcome that reluctance and to feel distinctly out of place in churches where there is no expectation of an encounter with the living God. Yet I have also witnessed an alarming self-absorption in the charismatic movement, alongside triumphalism, too great an emphasis on spiritual experience and a deep-rooted suspicion of anything resembling theological rigour. The quality of the movement's hymnody has also been patchy, to say the least—though in this regard the charismatics are hardly on their own.

Yet 'Follow me' leadership, by its very nature, requires a charismatic sensitivity—both the ability to trace the course of the pillar of cloud by day and the pillar of fire by night, and the God-given willingness and strength to go where the Spirit leads, regardless of personal cost and hardship. Praying at the beginning of each day that we might follow the promptings of the Spirit; taking time to listen to the still small voice that comforts, reassures, challenges and guides; meeting together with other Christians to discern where God is already at work so that we might become his 'fellow workers';[6] attending to dreams and visions and to prophets among us—those gifted with an unusual sensitivity to the way the wind is blowing: these appear to be essential activities for 'Follow me' leaders as they steer the narrow course between foolish gullibility on the one hand and soul-destroying scepticism on the other.

Such promptings of the Spirit of God can be dangerously subjective, of course, and must be rooted in and authenticated by the word of God. Otherwise we are in danger of being 'blown here and there by every wind of teaching and by the cunning and craftiness of people in their deceitful scheming' (Ephesians 4:14). Yet, without an awareness of the Spirit's presence, his guidance and his empowering, all leadership becomes in some way compromised. It's not surprising that the word 'charismatic', in secular parlance, has come to denote a man or woman whose leadership is fresh, attractive and inspiring.

We are not Jesus. It's an obvious point, but an important one with which to finish this chapter. Jesus, the 'pioneer and perfecter of our faith' was unique both in his life's calling and in the sheer depth of his obedience to the Father. He was also the Son of God. Yet the 'imitation of Christ' remains a worthy and honourable ambition, founded on the reality of the incarnation and on Jesus' call to 'follow me'. We too are to be pioneers, rooted yet free to follow the Spirit's leading. We too are to aim for perfection: 'Be perfect… as your heavenly Father is perfect' (Matthew 5:48). Yes, we remain fallen, blinkered, compromised and fallible, but that reality should spur us on to greater things, a vision of what could be, rather than breeding complacency and fatalism, a weary acceptance of what already is.

—— Part 3 ——

WAIT FOR ME

'Do not leave Jerusalem, but wait for the gift my Father promised.'

ACTS 1:4

LONG-TERM LEADERSHIP

One of the most remarkable features of Jesus' ministry was his ability to achieve so much in such a short time. Jesus was in his early to mid-30s when he died, and his active ministry lasted only three years, four at most. Yet the legacy of his life and teaching, his compassion and power, his death and resurrection, is simply incalculable. Even allowing for the uniqueness of Jesus' person and calling, there must be lessons here for us.

Why, we might wonder, did Jesus take so many years to launch his ministry? Why those hidden decades between his early child-hood and his late 20s, when we hear virtually nothing of him? And why, more surprisingly still, the small scale of his operation—weeks spent wandering from one little Galilean village to another, along-side the occasional trip to Jerusalem to celebrate Tabernacles or the Passover? It was hardly a worldwide ministry, we might think, hardly an attempt to take the Roman empire by storm.

Even within that narrow focus, there seems a curious approach to time management. Jesus never appeared rushed or hurried; why didn't he push himself harder? Why those occasions when he could have been out and about, teaching people, healing them, advancing the kingdom, but instead seemed to waste time hanging around in the desert or getting up early to pray? 'Everyone is looking for you!' exclaimed Simon and his companions after one such nocturnal prayer time, exasperated by Jesus' approach to time-keeping, yet Jesus wasn't willing to be dictated to by his disciples, the crowds or anyone else. 'Let us go somewhere else' was his somewhat abrupt response (Mark 1:36–38).

Perhaps a key to Jesus' effectiveness lies in the simple word

'Wait'. It is because he had discovered the secret of waiting on God, opening himself to God's direction and trusting in God's timing that the impact of his ministry could be so effective and enduring. 'Wait for the Lord' is a constant theme in the Psalms and the prophets; and Jesus had imbibed the Psalms and the prophets with his mother's milk.

The image of a child on a sunny day comes to mind—a child with a magnifying glass in his hand and a pile of leaves at his feet. If the child is constantly on the move, rushing from one place to another, the heat of the sun will make no impact on the leaves. But if the child stays still and begins to focus the sun's rays through the magnifying glass and on to just one leaf, it won't be long before that leaf catches fire—then another, and another. It's the stillness, the focus, the expectant waiting, that makes an impact, far more than the child's natural tendency to fidget or try to tackle the whole pile in one go.

Waiting can, of course, become an excuse for inaction, laziness, even fatalism. In Samuel Beckett's play *Waiting for Godot*,[1] the two tramps Vladimir and Estragon fill their days with increasingly meaningless chatter as they wait for someone who, if he comes (indeed, if he exists), will save them and fulfil their lives. 'Well, what shall we do?' asks Vladimir. 'Don't let's do anything,' replies his companion. 'It's safer.' The play touched a raw nerve on its first performance in 1954 and has continued to do so ever since, for the sheer passivity of the tramps in the face of a world that has lost touch with all but the faintest echo of meaning and purpose remains both bleak and curiously compelling.

Nothing, though, could be further removed from the biblical call to 'wait for the Lord' or from the faith-filled expectancy that lies at its heart. Waiting in this sense is both an active expression of our dependence on God and a recognition that his timing is not always our timing: that if we are to live (and lead) properly, we must do so for the long term rather than seeking first the quick win and a popularity that will evaporate as quickly as it has materialized. The wise man 'built his house on the rock', taught Jesus—a picture of hard work, patient work, carefully choosing the right foundation, the right materials and the right time. 'The rain came down, the streams rose, and the winds blew and beat against that house; yet it did not fall, because it had its foundation on the rock' (Matthew 7:24–25).

MISLEADERSHIP: SLEEPINESS AND IMPATIENCE

Simon Peter in the garden of Gethsemane provides us with a striking example of the misleadership that fails to take seriously the biblical injunction to 'wait for the Lord'. At one moment he was asleep, failing to support his Master in prayer just when Jesus was at his most desperate and distressed. At the next, awakened and dis-oriented, he grasped a sword and lashed out at one of the least significant members of the arrest party—the unassuming servant of the high priest whose name, writes John, was Malchus (John 18:10).

Sleepiness and impatience: an unlikely pairing, perhaps. But both in their different ways represent a rejection of the call to 'wait for the Lord'. Sleepiness may take waiting seriously but loses touch with the reason and purpose for the wait: think of Vladimir and Estragon, speaking out their increasingly incoherent thoughts as the faint memory of Godot becomes fainter still. Impatience may take the Lord seriously but removes waiting from the equation, just as Peter impulsively took matters into his own hands, seeking to achieve an arguably godly end through recourse to unarguably godless means. And whenever Jesus spoke of the need to wait, these twin temptations were never far away.

Of course, sleepiness is a universal phenomenon and is not, in itself, either sinful or faithless. It is easy to sympathize with Peter and his friends asleep in the garden following the emotional demands of the last supper, and Jesus in part shared that sympathy, admitting, 'The spirit is willing, but the flesh is weak' (Matthew 26:41). As a New Testament metaphor, though, sleepiness has wider and more negative connotations, and the Greek verb *gregoreo* (translated 'watch' in most Bible versions) contains at its heart the challenge to be on the ball and spiritually alert. Both the wise and the foolish virgins fell asleep as they waited for the coming of the bridegroom—there's nothing wrong with that—but only the wise virgins had truly 'watched'. Only they had remained alert, laying in extra supplies of oil so that they were ready when the big moment finally arrived (Matthew 25:1–13).

Of all the religious groupings in Jesus' day, it was the Sadducees who most personified the sleepiness of those foolish virgins. Generally well represented among the priestly and aristocratic classes, the Sadducees rejected talk of revolution and indeed of resurrection, preferring to focus on the worldly benefits that their prestige and privileges conferred upon them. All talk of watching and waiting, of the coming of God's kingdom or the return of the Son of Man, was entirely alien to such a self-satisfied worldview. (Even today it tends to be the dispossessed and poor that pray most fervently that ancient prayer, 'Maranatha. Come, Lord Jesus'.) And despite the early Church's unwavering commitment to the resurrection of Jesus from the dead, there were elements even among that community which seemed to mirror the Sadducees' complacency (see 1 Thessalonians 5:5–6; 2 Thessalonians 3:11–12).

'Understand this,' warned Jesus in response to this tendency: 'if the owner of the house had known at what time of night the thief was coming, he would have kept watch and would not have let his house be broken into. So you also must be ready, because the Son of Man will come at an hour when you do not expect him' (Matthew 24:43–44).

What of the opposite extreme, though? Peter lashing out at poor old Malchus? Again we see various traces of this through the Gospels, ranging from low-key domestic incidents to impatience on a grander, more nationalistic scale.

In the Sermon on the Mount, Jesus confronted the restlessness of the pagans, those who endlessly worry about what they will eat and drink and wear, and 'run after all these things' (Matthew 6:31–32). By contrast he called his disciples to a life focused on right priorities, a life of faith and contentment: 'Seek first his kingdom and his righteousness, and all these things will be given to you as well' (v. 33).

At other points in his ministry, too, Jesus found himself challenging his followers for their restlessness and impatience. In Luke 9, James and John (nicknamed the 'sons of thunder') had lightning on their minds when Jesus was given a hostile reception by a group of Samaritan villagers. 'Lord, do you want us to call fire down from heaven to destroy them?' was their question (v. 54), to which Jesus responded with a sharp rebuke. In the following chapter, Martha sought to take the situation in hand as her sister waited at the feet of Jesus: 'Lord, don't you care that my sister has left me to do the work by myself? Tell her to help me!' (10:40). Her words, too, attracted a reproof, though of a rather more gentle and affectionate nature. A little later on, Malchus' ear was miraculously healed as Jesus commanded Peter, 'Put your sword back in its place, for all who draw the sword will die by the sword' (Matthew 26:52).

There are also hints that Jesus was ministering against a backdrop of larger-scale impatience—the anger of many of his compatriots against the indignities (and not infrequent blasphemies) of Roman rule. While Jesus was growing up, a fellow Galilean named Judas stirred up a rebellion against Rome, which was brutally suppressed by the governor Quirinius.[2] During the governorship of Pontius Pilate, there were at least seven similar incidents, most of them sparked off by the procurator's bullish and tactless leadership style.[3] After Jesus' death, a new group arose, known as the Sicarii or 'Dagger-men', who specialized in raiding Jewish households and killing those they considered to be collaborators, and a series of revolts in the following years (including one led by an Egyptian Jew which attracted four thousand followers[4]) paved the way for the biggest uprising of them all: the Jewish War of AD66, which culminated in an appalling bloodbath and the destruction of the Jerusalem temple four years later.

There are legitimate doubts over the origins of the so-called 'Zealots' who were apparently responsible for these various events, and about whether they formed a single coherent group—Josephus' 'fourth sect' along with the Pharisees, the Sadducees and the Essenes.[5] There are also questions surrounding 'Simon the Zealot', one of the apostles called by Jesus (Mark 3:18). Was he part of this grouping or simply a generally enthusiastic and zealous character? But whatever the answers, the volatility of Israel in Jesus' day— organized or spontaneous—is indisputable. It formed the context for Jesus' attempts in the early stages of his ministry to keep his messianic identity a closely-guarded secret.[6] It found expression in the incident recorded in John 6, where Jesus, 'knowing that they intended to come and make him king by force, withdrew again to a mountain by himself' (v. 15). It helps to explain the fervour of the crowds on the first Palm Sunday and their later incomprehension when Jesus' next port of call brought judgment on the temple rather than Pilate's private residence; and following Jesus' death and resurrection, it raised the natural question, 'Lord, are you at this time going to restore the kingdom to Israel?' (Acts 1:6).

There is an occasional passage in the Gospels that could be read as advocating armed struggle,[7] but the overwhelming evidence points to Jesus' complete commitment to a policy of non-resistance and non-retaliation—walking the second mile, turning the other cheek. In Gethsemane he deliberately drew a contrast between his approach and that of his Zealot compatriots: 'Am I leading a rebellion, that you have come out with swords and clubs to capture me?' (Matthew 26:55). During his trial before Pilate, he stressed, 'My kingdom is not of this world. If it were, my servants would fight to prevent my arrest' (John 18:36). Through the scourging and mockery, on the road to Golgotha, as he hung upon the cross, Jesus' steadfast commitment to 'turn the other cheek' was put to its sternest and cruellest test.

The kingdom of God will not be advanced through the impatience of the Zealot. That is the message (or at least a message) of the cross. The ongoing temptation to achieve godly ends through godless means—to cut corners in the patient building of God's kingdom—must be resisted consistently and firmly, with even the well-meaning advice of a friend earning Jesus' vehement response, 'Get behind me, Satan!' (Matthew 16:23). Christians may remain divided on the rights and wrongs of armed resistance in the context of 'just war' theory, but there is no question that the Church's mission itself is not to be advanced by violent means. Latter day zealots remain a blot on the Christian landscape whenever persuasion is replaced by aggression, and encouragement by coercion.

Wise Christian leadership—'Wait for me' leadership—always includes the injunction to 'put away your sword'.

JESUS THE FARMER

In previous chapters, we have seen how Jesus' approachability as a 'Come to me' leader is well pictured in the biblical image of the gathering shepherd. Similarly, Hebrews' description of Jesus as the 'pioneer and perfecter of our faith' summarizes his unique abilities as an inspirational 'Follow me' leader. It is perhaps the picture of the farmer, though, that best picks up the theme of long-term leadership. 'Wait for me' recognizes the need to dig, to plant, to watch, to water, to be patient—and only then to reap the best of the crops, those that haven't been eaten, scorched or choked through the long months of apparent inactivity.

'Wait for me' acknowledges that times and seasons are God's idea, that 'as long as the earth endures, seedtime and harvest, cold and heat, summer and winter, day and night will never cease' (Genesis 8:22). Human attempts to subvert such creational rhythms in the quest for short-term prosperity will therefore prove counterproductive, ending in fruitlessness and exhaustion. And while this is not the place for some half-baked environmental thesis, it's clear that the absence of a 'Wait for me' element in the modern industrial psyche, and in the philosophy of all but the most visionary of the world's leaders, lies at the heart of many of our current environmental concerns. It is the dark side, perhaps, of the democratic dream, which all too easily places short-term popularity at the top of the political agenda.

The farmer, by contrast, takes a longer-term perspective on life. There is no sleepiness or inactivity in the way he goes about his work. Instead, considerable effort is needed as the land is prepared and the seed sown. In Jesus' famous parable of the sower (Matthew 13:1–9), we might perhaps question how thoroughly that preparatory work has been done: the man seems more concerned about getting the seed out there—spreading it far and wide—than he does about ensuring that stones and thorns are first removed and scarecrows constructed to keep the birds away. There's no question, though, of the hard work involved in the enterprise.

Yet then, the farmer has to wait. The seed can't be hurried along. The cycle of the seasons can't be altered. True, the farmer can do some watering and weeding (though even weeding doesn't seem too high in the farmer's priorities in Jesus' parable), but the need for patience, expectancy and trust is indisputable. As Paul wrote in a different context, 'I planted the seed, Apollos watered it, but God has been making it grow' (1 Corinthians 3:6).

And Jesus never explicitly identifies himself with the farmer in his parable. His focus is more on the seed and the soils than on the somewhat erratic, even wasteful, behaviour of the man doing the sowing. Yet much of Jesus' own experience is contained in this striking story.

As Jesus threw out the seed of God's kingdom, the response was patchy in the extreme, ranging from full-blown antagonism on the one hand to adoration, even worship, on the other. In between, there were some who responded enthusiastically for a while but fell away when the going got tough (John 6:66); while for others, the cost was just too high, such as the rich young man who 'went away sad, because he had great wealth' (Matthew 19:22). The kingdom of God might be at hand but the parable of the sower firmly rejects any idea of an instant, unanimous response on the part of God's people, let alone a decisive and triumphalistic victory over the forces of Roman oppression. Instead we have an agricultural picture of quiet growth, with many setbacks and disappointments along the way.

And the farmer in the parable is not obsessed with those setbacks: he is not rushing from field to field, pulling out thorns and chasing off birds in a burst of reactive activity. Rather, he trusts in the power of the seed, knowing that good seed planted in good soil will achieve a 30-fold, 60-fold, even 100-fold increase. Winston Churchill's definition of success as 'the ability to go from one failure to another with no loss of enthusiasm' may be somewhat tongue-in-cheek, but in many ways it sums up the attitude of Jesus' farmer—even, perhaps, of Jesus himself. There will be failures—Jesus' kingdom ministry, his words and actions, will fall on some pretty inhospitable terrain—but while battles are being lost, the war is being won. Such is the power of the kingdom seed at Jesus', and our, disposal.

What, then, are the characteristics of Jesus' 'Wait for me' leadership? Prayerful expectancy, proactivity, patience and endurance are key to its fruitfulness. There is nothing short-term about these qualities: the wise farmer who exhibits them may even look beyond his own lifetime for the fulfilment of the plans and aspirations that drive him. Yet, in a world that has so bought into the secular 'gospel' of short-term gain, it is vital that 'Wait for me' leaders model a different approach—the ability to work, watch and wait for the long-term, even eternal, benefit of those they lead and serve.

✛

THE CHARACTER OF THE FARMER

PRAYERFUL EXPECTANCY

'Do not leave Jerusalem,' instructed the risen Christ in the days leading up to Pentecost, 'but wait for the gift my Father promised, which you have heard me speak about.' And as they waited for the coming of the Spirit, the disciples 'joined together constantly in prayer, along with the women and Mary the mother of Jesus, and with his brothers' (Acts 1:4, 14).

In Chapter 3, we looked at Jesus' habit of withdrawing to a solitary place, his 'tent of meeting', a practice he maintained from the outset of his ministry in the Judean desert through to the eve of his death in the garden of Gethsemane. At times, as we have seen, this discipline kept his followers waiting, leaving them impatient at the priority Jesus gave to this unspectacular and apparently fruit-less activity. While Jesus was 'waiting for the Lord' in a positive, expectant manner, seeking the Father's direction, empowering and wisdom, the disciples were 'waiting for the Lord' in a far more ordinary sense—wondering when on earth Jesus was going to turn up. Yet gradually we witness a change in the men's attitude, brought about by a growing recognition of the centrality of prayer to Jesus' ministry and calling.

The disciples' failure to exorcise an evil spirit from a young boy and their disappointed question 'Why couldn't we drive it out?' prompted Jesus to respond, 'This kind can come out only by prayer' (Mark 9:28–29). And perhaps it was that incident, among others, that prompted the disciples to ask, 'Lord, teach us to pray', a re-quest which forms the backdrop to Jesus' magnificent teaching in

Luke 11: 'Ask and it will be given to you; seek and you will find; knock and the door will be opened to you... If you... know how to give good gifts to your children, how much more will your Father in heaven give the Holy Spirit to those who ask him!' (vv. 9, 13).

'Wait for the Lord': it's a challenge that could be given in a variety of contexts from the prosaic to the eschatological. Yet it's no coincidence that nearly half of the biblical references to this phrase are found in the Psalms, in the context of a living, trusting, prayerful relationship with the Almighty. Waiting in silence, waiting earnestly, waiting with hope: a number of Hebrew words pick up these various nuances, developing between them a rich devotional seam that runs throughout the Bible.

As the disciples waited in Jerusalem after Jesus' ascension, as they prepared to be 'clothed with power from on high' (Luke 24:49), they were therefore following in a long and honourable biblical tradition: 'In the morning, Lord, you hear my voice; in the morning I lay my requests before you and wait expectantly' (Psalm 5:3); 'I wait for the Lord more than watchmen wait for the morning' (130:6); 'They who wait for the Lord shall renew their strength; they shall mount up with wings like eagles; they shall run and not be weary; they shall walk and not faint' (Isaiah 40:31, ESV); 'It is good to wait quietly for the salvation of the Lord' (Lamentations 3:26).

Within a few years of Pentecost, the priority of this waiting would be built into the Christian week itself. Indeed, there's something serendipitous about the way the early Church changed its day of worship from Saturday, the last day of the week, to Sunday, the first day of the week.[1] Their primary motivation was to honour Jesus' resurrection from the dead on what became known as the 'Lord's Day' or the 'eighth day', but the effect of the change was to start the week with expectant worship before the paid employment of the following days began—a powerful visual aid, in terms of Isaiah 40:31, of the need to wait for the Lord before walking, running, and 'mounting up with wings like eagles'.

Psychologically and spiritually, this development remains highly significant. For working from a place of rest is quite different than resting from a place of work: it gives precedence to divine grace over human achievement. So, from the earliest days of the Church, the priority of expectant prayer, of waiting on God, of resting in his presence, was built into the Christian week itself.

PROACTIVITY

It wasn't simply Jesus' vibrant prayer life that kept his disciples waiting. There are many occasions in the Gospels when his timing and priorities seem poles apart from the expectations of those who surround him, as even the briefest look at the early part of Mark's Gospel makes clear.

In the opening chapter (as we have already noted), Simon's comment 'Everyone is looking for you' was met with the response, 'Let us go somewhere else!'—much to the surprise, I'm sure, of Simon and his colleagues, and the frustration of the excitable crowds. Three chapters on, we have the story of Jesus asleep in the boat while the storm rages around (4:37–38). His was not the sleep of escapism, as when the prophet Jonah dozed on the way to Joppa. It was rather the sleep of prayerful obedience, taking time to rest before attending (alarmingly late, so far as the disciples were concerned) to the raging wind and the waves.

In Mark 5 we read of the incident when Jesus delayed his visit to Jairus' daughter to respond to an unnamed woman with a haemorrhage. In the following chapter, Jesus, concerned for the well-being of his disciples, instructed them, 'Come with me by yourselves to a quiet place and get some rest' (6:31), although this time the crowds followed them around the lake so that the boat itself provided the only 'quiet place' available.

The most agonizing story of them all, however, is found not in Mark but in John 11—the emotionally charged account of the raising of Lazarus, where waiting plays a decisive part. Jesus heard of Lazarus' illness and almost inexplicably decided to remain where he was for two more days before going to visit his favourite family in Bethany. 'Lord, if you had been here, my brother would not have died' was the sisters' anguished response to his eventual arrival (vv. 21, 32).[2] 'Could not he who opened the eyes of the blind man have kept this man from dying?' was the reaction of those who'd come to share in their pain (v. 37). Yet Jesus knew what he was doing. Deeply moved by the grief both around him and within him, Jesus stood before the burial cave and cried in a loud voice, 'Lazarus, come out!' (v. 43). And the dead man emerged—the greatest miracle of them all prior to the glory of the first Easter morning.

It would be possible to regard such stories in a somewhat negative light. 'The person who can force another to wait has a particular power,' writes Hugh Rayment-Pickard. 'Indeed, keeping others waiting can be a way of "showing them who's boss".'[3] But this widespread abuse of 'Wait for me' authority is far removed from the servant leadership of Jesus. Instead we see a man whose prayerful commitment to 'wait for the Lord' enabled him consistently and skilfully to keep on track, to refocus his priorities, to reflect, listen and ponder rather than endlessly responding to multiple demands on his time and energy.

Such leadership is proactive at its heart, acknowledging the need to stand back and focus on the important more than the urgent. Such leaders frequently surprise those whom they lead by their clarity of vision, and equally confuse and disappoint those who demand a speedier pastoral responsiveness to their personal wants and needs. And while such an approach could become cold and calculating in the wrong hands, 'Wait for me' leadership at its best remains open to unexpected crises and pressing requests, but refuses to be driven by them. In terms of his encounter with the Canaanite woman (Matthew 15:21–28), Jesus' mission may be to feed the 'lost sheep of Israel', but there are still tasty crumbs left over for those who fall outside the scope of that fundamental calling.

'Be proactive' is the first of the 'seven habits of highly effective people' in Stephen Covey's multimillion bestseller of the same name, first published in 1990,[4] and it is confirmed as a key principle for church leaders in Bob Jackson's *Hope for the Church*[5] and *The Road to Growth*.[6] In the first of his books, Jackson created something of a stir by noting that the one place where the Church of England is experiencing substantial growth, London, is also the very place where requests for infant baptisms, weddings and funerals (so-called 'occasional offices') are at their fewest. Jackson was keen not to dismiss the value of such services out of hand, or their mission potential, but his research did expose a flaw in the 'traditional theory that the church is built by the pastoral contacts of the occasional offices'. 'Far from the church attendance tip of the Christendom iceberg melting away as underlying residual Christianity disappears,' Jackson concludes, 'the evidence suggests it might have a new chance to grow', as clergy and their congregations have 'more time, energy and focus available for building the gathered community of faith'.[7]

'Wait for me' leadership is therefore proactive leadership. To return to the image of the last chapter, it recognizes the futility of an attempt to light a whole bonfire at once, and instead stops to focus the heat of the sun on one leaf at a time.

PATIENCE

It wasn't just through his actions that Jesus lived out a 'Wait for me' approach. In his teaching, he often encouraged his followers to learn the lessons of the natural and agricultural worlds around them— lessons of a proper patience and trust in the timing and faithfulness of God.

Why was Jesus' ministry so patchy in its effectiveness? The parable of the sower, as we have seen, speaks of massive harvests but also many disappointments along the way. Why the apparent discrepancy between Jesus' grand talk of the 'kingdom of God' and the distinctly small-scale nature of his operations? The parable of the tiny mustard seed that 'becomes the largest of all garden plants' helps to explain his lack of anxiety on this score (Mark 4:30–32).

Why did Jesus seem equally unconcerned about the spiritual growth of those who heard his message? 'A man scatters seed on the ground,' he taught, a few verses earlier in Mark 4. 'Night and day, whether he sleeps or gets up, the seed sprouts and grows, though he does not know how' (vv. 26–27). And why was he so reluctant to 'weed' his disciples, to keep his followers pure? 'Do you want us to go and pull them up?' asked the servants in another agricultural parable (Matthew 13:24–30), as they viewed the weeds planted among the wheat. 'No,' was the response, 'because while you are pulling up the weeds, you may uproot the wheat with them.'

These are powerful images and important reminders to our culture, where an increasing detachment from the seasons and the agricultural year can all too easily create a restlessness in church life as much as society. ('What do we want?' 'Church growth!' 'When do we want it?' 'Now!') In pastoral terms, too, we can expect too much too soon—too much of ourselves as well as those we lead. Yet there are times, says Jesus, when we are called to exercise the patience to keep going and sowing, when our achievements seem very small and our progress very slow. We need patience, too, to allow certain situations in church life to remain unsatisfactory for a while, recognizing that to deal with them immediately may prove damaging and counter-productive. In Paul's words, we are not to 'grow weary in well-doing, for in due season we shall reap if we do not lose heart' (Galatians 6:9, RSV).

Of course, there can be a holy impatience, too—battering on the door of the next-door neighbour to get some food, in the image from that humorous parable of the friend at midnight (Luke 11:5–8). The same Spirit who comforts the disturbed persistently disturbs the comfortable, calling us away from the pseudo-patience of apathy and complacency or a stubborn refusal to contemplate necessary change.

Yet, provided we are waiting on God in prayer, and provided we are seeking to be proactive in throwing out the seed of the gospel as faithfully and imaginatively as we can, it is only right to leave the results to him. Any true work of God will take time to to put down roots, grow and bear fruit. Any true work will encompass the encouraging growth of spring, the flowering of summer, the necessary pruning of autumn and the fallow period of winter—the need, in God's terms, to 'wait for me'.

ENDURANCE

Patience in an agricultural sense might be seen as a necessary and relatively painless exercise—frustrating, perhaps, for those used to speedier results but not costly in any broader way. The Greek term *hupomone*, though, generally translated as 'perseverance' or 'patient endurance', reminds us that waiting can be both risky and painful, especially when lived out against a backdrop of suffering and persecution.

Hupomone literally means 'remaining under'—an ability to bear up courageously under the pressure of such sufferings—and it appears (in its verbal form) in verses such as Matthew 24:12–13: 'Because of the increase of wickedness, the love of most will grow cold, but whoever *stands firm* to the end will be saved.' In Hebrews 12:7, we are reminded that God can use such patient endurance for his purposes ('Endure hardship as discipline; God is treating you as his children'), while in the book of Revelation John describes himself as 'your brother and companion in the suffering and kingdom and patient endurance that are ours in Jesus Christ', before calling for 'patient endurance and faithfulness on the part of God's people' in the face of the beast and all his blasphemies (1:9; 13:10).

Hugh Rayment-Pickard helpfully coins the phrase 'apocalyptic time', which he identifies in terms of 'watching, hoping and waiting for a future revelation'. Apocalyptic time, he continues, 'is pregnant time, time orientated towards a disclosure to come'[8]; and pregnancy requires both patience and endurance, especially as it draws to a close and the labour pains set in. 'There will be earthquakes in various places, and famines,' teaches Jesus in Mark 13, about the end times and the return of the Son of Man. 'These are the beginnings of birth-pains' (v. 8). 'We know that the whole creation has been groaning as in the pains of childbirth right up to the present time,' writes Paul in Romans 8. 'Not only so, but we ourselves... groan inwardly as we wait eagerly for our adoption, the redemption of our bodies' (vv. 22–23).

Why, then, the pregnancy? Why the groaning? Romans 8 reminds us of the amazing destination to which our 'patient endurance' is leading—a transformation of the whole of creation, not simply of the individual believer. The groans of creation are not, as it might appear, its death throes, but are rather the shrieks of the delivery suite—equally painful, perhaps, yet far more positive and exciting in their final outcome.

Is the waiting itself, though, of any value, or is it simply a waste of time—like sitting at the traffic lights, something that we have to endure, either stoically or with a growing sense of anger and helpless frustration? Elsewhere in Romans, Paul makes this clear: 'We also glory in our sufferings, because we know that suffering produces perseverance [*hupomone*]; perseverance, character; and character, hope. And hope does not put us to shame, because God's love has been poured out into our hearts through the Holy Spirit, who has been given to us' (5:3–5).[9]

The early Christian apologists also pick up this theme and use the patient endurance of the Christian community (often in the face of the severest persecutions) as a powerful argument in favour of its trustworthiness and integrity. 'Have you not seen Christians flung to the wild beasts to make them deny their Lord, and yet remaining undefeated?' asks the anonymous author of the Epistle to Diognetus in around AD124. 'Do you not see how the more of them suffer such punishments, the larger grow the number of the rest? These things do not look like the work of man; they are the power of God, and the evident tokens of His presence.'[10]

And here, perhaps, is the heart of Jesus' 'Wait for me' leadership —a recognition that waiting itself can have real value in developing perseverance, character, hope and godly maturity[11] and, indeed, in growing the church as a whole. It's not that waiting is the only important thing (and here I have to take issue with Rayment-Pickard, who writes, 'Whether that revelation ever comes is beside the point'[12]), but waiting, and the 'patient endurance' that can accompany it, clearly play a key role in God's purposes and should be embraced as such.

In terms of his second coming, Jesus himself didn't know how long the wait would be: 'But about that day or hour no-one knows, not even the angels in heaven, nor the Son, but only the Father' (Matthew 24:36). All he could do was to urge his followers to be ready and vigilant, not sleepy like the Sadducees or impatient like the Zealots. And as the months have turned to years, the years to decades, the decades to centuries and the centuries to millennia, it has become ever more important to understand the purpose of waiting in God's plan of salvation. In the words of Peter, 'Do not forget this one thing, dear friends: with the Lord a day is like a thousand years, and a thousand years are like a day. The Lord is not slow in keeping his promise, as some understand slowness. Instead he is patient with you, not wanting anyone to perish, but everyone to come to repentance' (2 Peter 3:8–9).

JESUS' TRUST IN THE FATHER

Imagine someone walking into a church for the first time and picking up a copy of the New Testament. The front cover looks interesting. The blurb on the back makes some extraordinary claims. This book, it states, is not only the world's bestseller, but is also—wait for it—the word of God. Our newcomer turns the first page with a sense of growing expectation and reads the very first sentence: 'A record of the genealogy of Jesus Christ, the son of David, the son of Abraham'—followed by a list of 46 names, spelling out the family tree of this man, Jesus the Messiah.

Our newcomer (like most people) knows nothing of Aminadab or Salmon, Eliakim or Matthan, and he is frankly puzzled by such a prosaic start to something that purports to be a divinely inspired book. True, biographies of famous people often start a generation or two back, to help flesh out the family background of their subjects, but what possible influence can someone exercise over 40 generations? Why not start with Mary and Joseph (who eventually pop up as numbers 45 and 46 on the list) and have done with it?

One answer that occurs to our newcomer is that the author of the book is simply a man who likes his family trees—a genealogy bore. There has, after all, been a popular explosion of interest in our forebears in recent times, complete with the proliferation of relevant websites and a whole raft of books and programmes tracing the history of individual people, houses, villages and cities. Perhaps there were similar trends around when this book was written. Maybe the author, had he lived today, would have spent much of his time glued in front of a computer and trawling his way through www.familytree.com.

As our reader begins to think more deeply, though, another possible answer presents itself. The building into which he or she has walked is a medieval church and is set in the midst of a rural community near the sea. There are plaques on the walls and gravestones in the churchyard, which indicate the leading families that have lived out their days in that place—the Westcots and the Winters, the Stuckleys and the Syncockes—generations and generations of them. Our newcomer—a Londoner—imagines being a medieval farmer in those parts, and pictures the strength of the generational links that bind that farmer to both his ancestors and his successors. The orchard that the farmer plants today will be for the benefit of his children and his children's children. The god of that farmer—the values and belief systems that he holds dear—will similarly be passed from one generation to the next, like the baton in a relay race.

And Matthew's interest in Jesus' family tree reflects this interrelated understanding of human history, providing us with a fascinating insight into the family in which Jesus was born and raised. For one thing, it is clear that the family is linked to some of the most impressive characters in the story of Israel, Abraham and David among them.[1] For another, there is a quirkiness to the list— especially where it focuses on abnormal incidents like the liaisons between Judah and Tamar, Rahab and Boaz, David and Bathsheba[2] —which arguably helps to prepare his readers for the unusual account of Jesus' conception and the virgin birth.

Yet it's the culmination of the genealogy that perhaps causes the greatest surprise: 'Jacob [was] the father of Joseph, the husband of Mary, and Mary was the mother of Jesus who is called the Messiah' (1:16). After all those 42 generations, we finally come to Jesus, only to discover that, in a strictly biological sense, he was not related to these people at all. Is this perhaps an embarrassment to Matthew, a little point that he hopes he can quietly gloss over? Or does it rather contain two remarkable new insights: first, that our spiritual forebears may sometimes be more significant than our physical forebears, and second, that the birth of Jesus marks a decisive break in the history of Israel?

Both of these insights are fleshed out further in the Gospels, not least by John the Baptist, who challenges his hearers, 'Do not think you can say to yourselves, "We have Abraham as our father." I tell you that out of these stones God can raise up children for Abraham. The axe has been laid to the root of the trees, and every tree that does not produce good fruit will be cut down and thrown into the fire' (Matthew 3:9–10).[3] Yet the opening of Matthew's Gospel suggests that the discontinuity of the virgin birth is not the whole story—that there's another sense in which Jesus is continuing in the line and ministry of his spiritual forebears, bringing the story of Abraham and Isaac and Jacob to a fitting conclusion, while simultaneously opening up new vistas in God's plan of salvation. Indeed, Abraham, Isaac and Jacob are still living, according to Jesus in his dispute with the Sadducees about the reality of the resurrection, for God is 'not the God of the dead but of the living' (Matthew 22:32).

So who are Jesus' successors in Matthew's Gospel? Whose name should appear in the 43rd generation after Abraham, following the words, 'And Jesus was the father of…'? Certainly not a lovechild from a fictitious liaison with Mary Magdalene, despite the runaway success of Dan Brown's *The Da Vinci Code*![4] Rather, we should focus on the somewhat motley collection of disciples who gather on a Galilean mountain in Matthew 28 to receive the Great Commission: 'Go and make disciples of all nations' (v. 19).

If life is a relay, then—if the opening verses of Matthew's Gospel chart the somewhat bumpy progress of 42 generations of runners from Abraham through to Jesus the Messiah—two implications follow.

First, the idea of preparation—the years at the beginning of our lives where we effectively 'get up to speed'—should be seen in a new light. The 75 years before Abram was called by God, the 80 years preceding Moses' encounter at the burning bush, the 30 years of Jesus' own short life spent in relative obscurity: all these make a great deal more sense when set against the backdrop of a plan of salvation that grows and develops from one generation to the next.

A person who decides to pitch a tent will not need to bother about digging out its foundations: the tent is only a temporary structure and is hardly expected to remain where it is for more than a week or two. A person who decides to build a mighty temple is in a different position. Great amounts of time and trouble need to go into its foundations: they need to be tested to the absolute limit. And the church, writes Paul, is 'built on the foundation of the apostles and prophets, with Christ Jesus himself as the chief corner-stone' (Ephesians 2:20).

The second implication is that if preparation at the beginning of the lap is crucial, equally critical is the handover at its end. No longer should I view my achievements (or indeed my failings) in isolation from those of generations yet to come. No longer should my legacy be seen purely in terms of what I manage to fit into the 40 or 70 or 100 years allotted to me. Instead, my job is to complete my stint as faithfully and fruitfully as I can while seeking to ensure a smooth and effective passing of the baton to my spiritual successors.

This is a principle that I've seen lived out on many occasions, most recently in the death of Penny Phillips, an extravert drama teacher in our church, following a courageous three-year fight with leukaemia. My funeral sermon on that occasion largely wrote itself: for the most part I simply read a number of emails in which Penny charted the highs and lows of her illness and her faith, with an honesty and a humour that were refreshing and deeply inspiring. And as I looked across the church to her husband, to their three sons who are all involved in Christian ministry, and to the generations of Penny's students who packed out the building that day, I was struck afresh by the image of the baton, the spiritual legacy that Penny had passed on so fruitfully and effectively. 'For what is our hope, our joy, or the crown in which we will glory in the presence of our Lord Jesus when he comes?' Paul wrote to the Thessalonian Christians: 'Is it not you?' (1 Thessalonians 2:19).

The essence of all this is the little word 'trust'. We need to trust in the love and faithfulness of God himself, most especially in times of testing, and trust that, despite all evidence to the contrary, 'God is working his purpose out as year succeeds to year'[5]—indeed, as millennium succeeds to millennium. Without such trust, we give way either to the sleepy incoherence of a Vladimir or Estragon or to the impulsive violence of a sword-wielding Simon Peter. Without such trust, we all too easily lose hope.

The story of the exodus includes the images of the tent of meeting, the tablets of stone and the pillars of cloud and fire, images upon which we have drawn in Chapters 3 and 7. But it is the desert —that barren and challenging environment in which the people of Israel spent 40 long years—that provides a powerful metaphor for the 'Wait for me' leader.

The desert was, in part, a place where God punished his people after their faithless response to the return of the spies from the 'land flowing with milk and honey'.[6] 'For forty years I was angry with that generation…' God said through the psalmist. 'So I declared on oath in my anger, "They shall never enter my rest"' (Psalm 95:10–11).

The desert was also, though, a place of discipline in a more positive and forward-looking sense, 'to humble and test you in order to know what was in your heart' (Deuteronomy 8:2). God the master craftsman was rebuilding the foundations of the nation of Israel and testing them to their limits.

More positive still are the frequent references to God's provision during the 40 years of waiting: 'The Lord your God has blessed you in all the work of your hands. He has watched over your journey through this vast wilderness. These forty years the Lord your God has been with you, and you have not lacked anything' (2:7).[7]

And most positively of all, the picture of the desert as the perfect destination for a second honeymoon is picked up by the prophet Hosea: 'Therefore I am now going to allure her,' says God about his faithless people; 'I will lead her into the wilderness and speak tenderly to her… There she will respond as in the days of her youth, as in the day she came up out of Egypt' (Hosea 2:14–15).

The idea that one experience can be simultaneously a punishment, a discipline, a blessing and a honeymoon is somewhat unusual but it illustrates succinctly Paul's claim in Romans 8:28: 'We know that in all things God works for the good of those who love him, who have been called according to his purpose'. Waiting is clearly a mixed experience for those called to practise it, but trust is at its heart—rebuilding trust after past lapses, growing in trust through present-day dependence and building (and testing) trustworthy foundations for the future.

Of course, when Jesus was driven into the wilderness, it was not as a punishment for past misdeeds. 'This is my Son, whom I love; with him I am well pleased' were the words ringing in his ears as he began his 40 days of fasting and waiting (Matthew 3:17)—words that contain a faint echo of Genesis 1:31, where God looked on his newly created humanity and proclaimed it 'very good' (v. 31). If the wilderness was, in any sense, a punishment for Jesus, that could only be seen in the context of his ongoing identification with sinful human beings—an identification that began with his baptism[8] and culminated on the cross.

Yet, for Jesus, those 40 days in the wilderness were a time of discipline, endurance, patience and, above all, trust-building. Thrown into a situation where he had no food, no companions, no timetable, no status, nothing (at least obviously) to achieve, the only two responses open to Jesus were to trust or to panic.

Trust, by its nature, suggests that the situation we are facing is uncertain and in some senses outside our control. Faith, as the writer to the Hebrews puts it, 'is being sure of what we hope for and certain of what we do not see' (11:1). If the world were a place of unmitigated beauty and pleasure—if we and our fellow human beings were characterized by utter faithfulness and complete integrity—there would be no need for trust.

'Do not worry about your life, what you will eat or drink; or about your body, what you will wear,' Jesus would shortly be teaching. 'For the pagans run after all these things, and your heavenly Father knows that you need them' (Matthew 6:25, 32). At face value this might sound like a charming sentiment, suitable for inclusion in one of those anthologies of calming quotations. But in reality, such radical trust is far from sentimental. It could only be formed in a place of uncertainty, a place where the basic bene-volence of the world (and indeed of God himself) was far from clear. Jesus' famous sermon might have been proclaimed on the mountain but the sermon preparation took place in the desert.

If the need for trust were evident in the wilderness, how much more would it become so as Calvary increasingly cast its shadow across Jesus' path. In John's Gospel, the sense of waiting for an impending crisis is picked up in several variations on the phrase, 'My hour has not yet come' (see, for example, 2:4; 7:6, 30; 8:20). After the triumphal entry into Jerusalem, Jesus dramatically announced, 'The hour *has* come for the Son of Man to be glorified' (12:23) and, in the first inklings of the agony in the garden of Gethsemane, he continued, 'Now my heart is troubled, and what shall I say? "Father, save me from this hour"? No, it was for this very reason I came to this hour. Father, glorify your name!' (vv. 27–28).

In easier times, Jesus had taught the goodness of God in terms of a father giving good gifts to his children. 'Which of you fathers,' he'd said, 'if your son asks for a fish, will give him a snake instead? Or if he asks for an egg, will give him a scorpion?' (Luke 11:11–12). On Calvary, that teaching would be tested to his limit, as snakes and scorpions, the 'sting of death', seemed far more in evidence than fish and eggs, the stuff of life. Yet once again it is the long-term nature of God's plan of salvation—a plan begun in the days of Abraham, Isaac and Jacob, continued through the faithful witness of women like Ruth and men like David, and supremely fulfilled through the death of Jesus—that helps to explain this apparent conundrum.

Looking towards his successors—the '43rd generation' in Matthew's genealogy—Jesus picked up another agricultural image as his hour arrived: 'Unless a grain of wheat falls to the ground and dies, it remains only a single seed. But if it dies, it produces many seeds' (John 12:24). Reflecting on God's family, with the benefit of post-resurrection hindsight, the writer to the Hebrews concluded, 'Jesus is not ashamed to call them brothers and sisters', and then, shifting the image from brother to father, he put the words of Isaiah on Jesus' lips: 'Here I am, and the children God has given me' (Hebrews 2:11, 13; see Isaiah 8:18).

✛

—————— 12 ——————

EMBRACING THE CALL
TO PASSIONATE PATIENCE

It was always going to be an awkward evening. The bishop had come to the meeting to tell the small congregation that St Saviour's was no longer viable and that there were only two options open to them. One was closure—the dispersal of the congregation and the conversion of their building into flats. The other was a so-called 'church plant'—an invitation to a thriving church nearby to send 50 of its members to start something new, with all the disruption and change that that would inevitably involve.

The idea of a 'church plant' sounded threatening to the congregation as the bishop spelt out the details. No longer would St Saviour's consist of a gentle group of people who had known each other for decades. No longer would their liturgy or hymnody go unquestioned. The bishop's vision was being met with all the enthusiasm of a small Northumbrian village in the ninth century being told to expect a wave of Vikings at any moment. While rape and pillage were not on the agenda, references to 'happy-clappy' worshippers and 'Bible-bashing fundamentalists' most definitely were.

The outcome of the meeting seemed sad but inevitable: the congregation would prefer their church to be closed than invaded. The kettle was on, the biscuits were ready, and it was about time for the business of the evening to draw to a close. Then Joan, an 86-year-old churchwarden, spoke up: 'I've been a member of this church for 60 years, and in all that time we've never made the slightest impact on our community. Tonight is our big chance!' And as she continued speaking, other members of the congregation began to nod in agreement as the vision of change and growth began to prevail over the vision of decline and death.

The 'Vikings' duly arrived and were found to be surprisingly friendly; the church community was saved, and is currently a couple of hundred people strong. All the original congregation remain as part of the new St Saviour's—all except Joan, who died just three weeks after the meeting, having secured the future of the church that she'd served and loved over all those years. At her funeral, the words of another great 'waiter', the old man Simeon, took on a special new resonance: 'Lord, now lettest thou thy servant depart in peace, according to thy word' (Luke 2:29, KJV).

In past chapters we have considered Jesus' own example of waiting on the Lord and, in turn, of expecting his followers to wait for him, but the rest of the New Testament and the course of human history clearly indicate that the call both to wait and (on occasions) to keep others waiting is intrinsic to leadership as a whole, not simply to the leadership of Jesus.

After Jesus' ascension—just at a time when Peter must have been itching to prove his leadership credentials—the Lord's clear instruction was that the disciples were to wait in Jerusalem (Acts 1:4). Opinion is divided as to whether Peter should have used those ten days of waiting to find a replacement for Judas (vv. 21–26): it might have been sensible to leave that decision until after the coming of the Spirit rather than resorting to the old expedient of casting lots. It's clear from Acts 1, however, that the majority of the time was spent in expectant prayer rather than frenetic activity—waiting on the Lord preceding walking, running and 'soaring on wings like eagles' (Isaiah 40:31).

The apostle Paul was called to a time of waiting soon after his experience on the road to Damascus. Luke tells us how quickly he jumped into action following that encounter: 'At once he began to teach in the synagogues that Jesus is the Son of God' (Acts 9:20). But it is left to Paul himself to describe the aftermath of that typically activist start to his Christian ministry: 'I did not go up to Jerusalem to see those who were apostles before I was, but I went into Arabia'— where he seems to have stayed for three years before returning to active ministry (Galatians 1:17–18). Quite what he did during that time remains a mystery: John Stott writes, 'It has even be suggested that those three years in Arabia were a deliberate compensation for the three years of instruction which Jesus gave the other apostles, but which Paul missed'.[1] Yet how wise it was of Paul to recognize the need for a long period of solitude to work through the implications of his life-changing encounter with the risen Christ.

The book of Acts and the remainder of the New Testament contain a number of further stories of enforced waiting, to which the apostles appear to have responded with extraordinary wisdom and grace. Periods in prison provided opportunities to worship God, to experience his miraculous intervention, to write epistles and to witness to jailers and fellow prisoners alike (see Acts 12:5–10; 16:25–34; Ephesians 6:19–20; Philippians 1:12–14). Showcase trials gave defendants the right to proclaim Christ to some of the key leaders of their day, with one of them (King Agrippa) responding to the passion of Paul's defence with the question, 'Do you think that in such a short time you can persuade me to be a Christian?' (Acts 26:28). A period of incarceration on a boat bound for Rome provided Paul with an opportunity to save many lives, earning himself the right to preach and heal significant numbers on the island of Malta (27:27—28:10),[2] while John's exile on the island of Patmos provided the setting for the visions of the book of Revelation, which have continued to bring hope and nourishment to the persecuted church over the past two millennia.

Sickness, too, could open the way to fresh revelation, if, as it seems, Paul's 'thorn in the flesh' was a medical condition of some kind.[3] We use the word 'patient' in English to describe someone who is ill (generously giving the benefit of the doubt to those whose approach to illness is impatient in the extreme), and 2 Corinthians 12:8 finds Paul as one such patient, praying on three occasions for his 'thorn in the flesh' to be taken away, apparently to no avail. Rather than giving way to doubt and self-pity in the face of such struggles, the apostle came to recognize that the 'thorn' was playing an important part in his life and ministry, keeping him humble and revealing to him that most significant of insights—that God's grace was sufficient for him and that 'when I am weak, then I am strong' (v. 10).

Patience is a feature (in a somewhat different sense) of the book of Hebrews. 'We do not want you to become lazy,' writes the author, 'but to imitate those who through faith and patience inherit what has been promised' (6:12). The inspiring list of the heroes of faith in Hebrews 11 provides the supreme illustration of the long-term nature of God's plan of salvation: 'All these people were still living by faith when they died. They did not receive the things promised... Instead, they were longing for a better country—a heavenly one. Therefore God is not ashamed to be called their God, for he has prepared a city for them' (vv. 13, 16).

And perhaps the story of Joan, the churchwarden whose last-minute intervention opened the way for our second church plant at St Saviour's, Sunbury, is not entirely out of place in such exalted company. Joan could hardly be accused of impatience: 60 years of belonging to a church that had 'never made any impact' on its community might well be regarded as erring on the opposite side. Yet the fact that Joan (as we later discovered) had been praying for the church's renewal over those 60 years, as well as the enthusiasm with which she embraced the idea of a church plant when it finally arose, seem to speak of the watchfulness and wakefulness that have characterized the 'wise bridesmaids' of every generation (see Matthew 25:1–13).

PUTTING THE WAITING BACK INTO WANTING

Given such a 'great cloud of witnesses' to the significance of this long-term vision, given Jesus' consistent use of agricultural metaphors to stress the need for patience in the face of the religious zealotry of his day, and given the need for the Church of Christ to be built with strong foundations and with the very best of building materials (see 1 Corinthians 3:10–15), it should go without saying that Christian leaders are called to eschew short-termism and to recognize both their indebtedness to their spiritual forebears and their responsibility to those who come after them. They are called to run their own lap with faithfulness and fruitfulness but always with an eye to the long-term blessing of the communities they serve.

Our spiritual forebears constructed a thousand churches and chapels and abbeys and cathedrals to God's glory, often employing the foremost builders and craftsmen of their time, inspired by the sense of a legacy that would transcend both time and the somewhat humble environments in which those mighty buildings were first erected. While their motivation was no doubt complex, and while buildings themselves can often prove a mixed blessing to those who inherit them, our forebears certainly displayed a confidence in both the extent and the long-term nature of the Church's mission.

Here, however, we hit a problem—the problem of the profoundly short-term culture in which we live and move and have our being. It was in 1972 that Access, the first widely available credit card, was issued under the slogan, 'Take the waiting out of wanting', and the intervening years have witnessed an extraordinary flowering of this short-term philosophy in industry, politics, commerce and the soundbite culture of today's media. Christian believers—and those who lead them—are born and raised in such an environment, and the consequence of such short-term thinking (especially in cities and suburbs where people are almost entirely detached from the norms of agricultural life and the cycle of the seasons) can be deeply frustrating.

The truth is that, all too often, Christian leaders have no idea how to connect the long-term message of God's plan of salvation to a short-term culture that seems entirely uninterested in anything beyond a temporary 'feel-good' vibe. As a result, they move in one of two directions—either towards an escapist determination to keep things exactly as they always have been, in the increasingly vain hope that the culture will move towards the church if the church steadfastly refuses to move towards the culture; or else towards a burst of manic activity that seeks to match the surrounding short-termism with its own brand of 'feel-good' spirituality. There are even churches and leaders that move from one extreme to the other, like Simon Peter in the garden of Gethsemane, waking from head-in-the-sand escapism and then lashing out in headless-chicken activism. The process can be reversed, too, as increasingly fruitless activity drifts into the cynicism and apathy of pastoral burnout.

Eugene Peterson provides us with an excellent diagnosis of this kind of approach and begins to point to a possible cure. Writing on the importance of the book of Revelation to pastoral ministry, he poses the following question.

If everything is falling apart, and the world is coming to an end, doesn't that mean the end of patience? Why not cut and run? Why not eat, drink and be merry for tomorrow we die? Bastard apocalyptic, apocalyptic that has no parentage in biblical sources or gospel commitments, does produce a progeny of irresponsibility (and the brats are noisily and distressingly in evidence on every American street).

Peterson then writes of the contrast:

The real thing, the conceived-in-wedlock apocalyptic, develops communities that are passionately patient, courageously committed to work and witness in the kingdom of God, no matter how long it takes, or how much it costs… The reason St John insists on patience is that he is dealing with the vast mysteries of God and the intricacies of the messy human condition. This is going to take some time. Neither the mysteries nor the mess is simple. If we are going to learn a life of holiness in the mess of history, we are going to have to prepare for something intergenerational and think in centuries.

[Yet] the working environment of pastors erodes patience and rewards impatience. People are uncomfortable with mystery (God) and mess (themselves). They avoid both mystery and mess by devising programmes and hiring pastors to manage them. A programme provides a defined structure with an achievable goal. Mystery and mess are eliminated at a stroke.[4]

It's a powerful thesis, and rings all too true to those involved in church leadership. Peterson's programme-ridden church is in danger of becoming a somewhat sanitized version of the heresy of the Zealots—the idea that the purposes of God can be nicely pushed along by our own little schemes, even where corners have to be cut and gospel values sacrificed in order to move the organization on. Gone is the patience of the sower who flings out the seed but trusts God for the outcome. Gone is the patience of the master who allows the wheat and weeds to grow together in a messy fashion, rather than wading in to try to sort everything out. Gone is any sense that 'God is working his purpose out as year succeeds to year'. Instead we succumb to our credit card culture—'taking the waiting out of wanting'—and worship impatience. Impatience, writes Peterson, 'the refusal to endure, is to pastoral character what strip mining is to the land—a greedy rape of what can be gotten at the least cost, and then abandonment in search of another place to loot.'[5]

Yet if 'passionate patience' is the cure to this disease, if God is truly calling the Church and its leadership to be 'courageously committed to work and witness in the kingdom of God, no matter how long it takes, or how much it costs',[6] how do we get from here to there?

The answer, as we have already suggested, is to be found in the desert.

THE DESERT

When I first started writing this book, I was concerned that the images of the tent of meeting and of the desert were rather too similar, for both involved withdrawing from the world of activity and seeking God in a place of intimacy and contemplation. There is one startling difference between the two images, however, which is that the desert experience, unlike that of the tent, is largely involuntary. Israel was taken into the desert and forced to remain there for 40 long years. Jesus was driven into the desert by the powerful wind of the Spirit of God. Even when God spoke through Hosea of his longing to lead his people back into the desert and speak tenderly to them, that leading was not to be voluntary on the part of the people: it would be brought about by the Assyrian army, who would shortly sweep into the northern kingdom and take the Israelites into enforced exile.

Exile, persecution, sickness, pregnancy and childbirth, seemingly intractable family relationships, traffic jams: all to varying extents share the sense of powerlessness, the recognition that we no longer call the shots. Even 'waiting for the Lord' clearly implies that we're no longer in control, that the wait may be uncomfortably extended, and for those who are accustomed to running their own lives, it's the powerlessness of waiting that makes it such a deeply frustrating and even panicky experience. Yet there is a strong but frequently neglected strand in the New Testament record that encourages us to embrace the desert with enthusiasm, even joy (see, for example, Romans 5:3–4; James 1:2–4; 1 Peter 1:7). For God's ability to bring about genuine transformation in our lives is severely limited when we are in control (this is the dark side, if you like, of his precious gift of free will), while our times of personal powerlessness provide precisely the opportunity for the transforming power of God to get to work on us, building strong foundations on which a genuine, fruitful, long-term life and ministry can be securely based.

'Imagine yourself as a living house,' writes C.S. Lewis:

God comes in to rebuild that house. At first, perhaps, you can understand what he is doing. He is getting the drains right and stopping the leaks in the roof and so on: you knew that those jobs needed doing and so you are not surprised. But presently he starts knocking the house about in a way that hurts abominably and does not seem to make sense. What on earth is he up to? The explanation is that he is building quite a different house from the one you thought of—throwing out a new wing here, putting on an extra floor there, running up towers, making courtyards. You thought you were going to be made into a decent little cottage: but he is building a palace. He intends to come and live in it himself.[7]

How, then, do we respond to the challenges that life (or, dare we say it, God) throws at us? Do we respond with predictable impatience, frustration, even rage; or do we accept the desert, embrace it—even, in the words of James 1:2, 'consider it pure joy'—because of the fruit it can produce within us? What might appear to be somewhat marginal questions are suddenly revealed as extraordinarily significant, for these are the 'Wait for me' questions that will largely determine the long-term effectiveness of our ministry.

In Chapter 8, I mentioned a trip to China in which I was privileged to meet Pastor M and his wife. The visit was, in part, an opportunity to witness for myself the extraordinary growth of the church in both its official and its unofficial manifestations, but it was also something of a family odyssey, retracing the steps of my grandparents, who lived and worked as medical missionaries from 1924 to 1939.

For most of that time, their home was in Kunming, the capital of Yunnan province in the south-west of the country, and that was our first main destination after flying to Beijing. My highly experienced travelling companion introduced me to a number of the church leaders in the city, and it was an honour to attend my grandparents' old church (which was bursting at the seams) and to speak at a number of more informal house churches, meeting in flats and factory compounds. Later, back in Beijing, we stumbled across an elderly woman who had been my grandfather's deputy between 1935 and 1938 (an extraordinary story that I later contributed to John Woolmer's book *Encounters*).[8]

When my grandparents were forced to leave China during the Sino-Japanese War (returning to east London, where my grandfather went on to lead the Mildmay hospital through the Blitz and beyond), the number of Christians in Yunnan was comparatively few. Communist Party researchers estimate that even by 1950 (eleven years later) there were only around 100,000 Christians across the whole enormous province—a figure that could so easily have been decimated by the appalling persecutions of the Mao era.

In fact, the Maoist 'desert' proved to be a time of near miraculous growth for the Chinese church, although my grandfather died too early to witness it. By 1996, the official figure in Yunnan had grown to 800,000 believers, a figure that excluded every Christian under the age of 18 and a very large number of unregistered members in the burgeoning house churches. Some of the minority groups, in particular, had experienced an extraordinary spiritual revival, especially the Lisu, Miao, Yi and Lingpo peoples. Today the figure of Christian believers is significantly higher still, and continues to increase year on year.[9]

Self-evidently, my grandparents were but two among many hundreds of faithful men and women who went to live and preach the good news of Jesus in Yunnan and beyond. But little could they have imagined the significance and effectiveness of their efforts as they faithfully ran their lap of the great kingdom race before handing over the baton to the many successors whose lives they had touched and inspired.

—— Part 4 ——

GO FOR ME

'All authority in heaven and on earth has been given to me. Therefore go and make disciples of all nations.'

MATTHEW 28:18–19

✛

MULTIPLYING LEADERSHIP

One of the most fascinating documents to come down to us from the early second century AD was a letter written by Pliny to the Roman Emperor Trajan. Sent as an ambassador to Bithynia in northern Asia Minor, Pliny was astonished to find a thriving church in the province, and determined to write to the emperor for advice and guidance. Pliny wrote of how the Christians

... maintained that they had met regularly before dawn on a fixed day to chant verses alternately amongst themselves in honour of Christ as if to a god, and also to bind themselves by oath, not for any criminal purpose, but to abstain from theft, robbery, adultery, to commit no breach of trust and not to deny a deposit when called upon to restore it. After this ceremony it had been the custom to disperse and reassemble later to take food of an ordinary, harmless kind; but they had in fact given up this practice since my edict, issued on your instructions, which banned all political societies. This made me decide that it was all the more necessary to extract the truth by torture from two slave women, whom they call deaconesses. I found nothing but a degenerate sort of cult carried to extravagant lengths.

I therefore adjourned the case and hastened to consult you. The matter seemed to me worth deliberation, especially on account of the number of those in danger. A great many individuals of every age and class, both men and women, are being brought to trial, and this is likely to continue. It is not only the towns, but villages and rural districts too which are infected through contact with this wretched cult. Yet it seems possible to stop it and set it right. There is no doubt that people have begun to throng the temples which had been almost entirely deserted for a long time; the sacred rites which had been allowed to lapse are being performed again, and flesh of sacrificial victims is on sale everywhere, though up till recently scarcely anyone could be found to buy it.[1]

This letter (written in around AD112) gives us real insights into the simple worship of the early church, the high ethical standards to which the believers aspired and the ongoing persecution that accompanied the church's growth and development. Pliny seems to have accepted that some of the wilder rumours about the Christians were unfounded (the widespread idea that they practised cannibalism, for example, may underlie his emphasis on 'food of an ordinary, harmless kind') but overall his verdict was clear: the early Church was a 'wretched cult'—even, more dangerously, a 'political society'—that paid allegiance to Christ rather than Caesar and therefore needed to be suppressed by all possible means.

Perhaps the letter's most striking feature, though, is Pliny's reference to the breadth of the early Church's appeal, reaching out to 'many individuals of every age and class', to men and women, and to towns, villages and rural districts alike. This had clearly sparked off a renewed interest in pagan religion, too, as the challenge of the gospel cut through the apathy of its day, forcing people to come off the religious fence one way or the other. Yet Pliny appeared confident that the temples would win out in the end, especially when helped along by some judicious persecution of their 'degenerate' rivals.

This is just one document, of course, but Pliny's letter takes its place among a number of accounts, Christian, Jewish and Roman, charting the extraordinary spread of the early church in the first hundred years of its existence.[2] The missionary fervour and fruitfulness of those early Christians was simply unique in the history of civilization up to that point, and so was the inclusiveness of their message of salvation, embracing alike both Jew and Gentile, Greek and barbarian, rich and poor, the oppressed and the oppressor, the sinner and the devout. 'It was a movement,' writes David Bosch, 'without analogy, indeed a sociological impossibility'.[3] No wonder it caused such a stir in the mighty Roman empire, rapidly earning for itself the designation 'the third race' on the streets of Carthage,[4] and the label of 'a new and malevolent superstition' on the lips of the prominent Roman historian Suetonius.[5]

Looking at the origins of the Christian faith, and its foundations in the religion of Israel, it is especially surprising that the first worldwide missionary movement should emanate from such a source. It's true that a prophet like Jonah could be sent out as a kind of missionary to the city of Nineveh, though only to announce its doom. It's true, more positively, that the prophecies of Isaiah contain the vision of a missionary God who will reveal his glory to the Gentiles, draw them in to worship him, and even invite them to partake in the messianic banquet (see, for example, 18:7; 25:6–8; 40:5; 42:6; 51:5). But to quote Bosch again, 'There is, in the Old Testament, no indication of believers of the old covenant being sent by God to cross geographical, religious, and social frontiers in order to win others to faith in Yahweh... The decisive difference between the Old and New Testament is mission'.[6]

And here is where we come to our fourth and final leadership phrase: 'Go for me'. For the command to 'Go!' is one of the most distinctive and revolutionary features of Jesus' ministry, creating the dynamic of multiplication that so unsettled Pliny and his Roman contemporaries. The missionary thrust of the Church didn't start with the first Good Friday or Easter morning, the day of Pentecost (Acts 2:1–4) or the conversion of Saul (9:1–19), the foundation of the church of Antioch (11:19–21) or the council of Jerusalem (15:1–21), although these were all key markers along the way (and the first three, at least, utterly essential). The root of the Church's missionary vision lay first in the practice and teaching of Jesus himself and in a theology of the kingdom of God that had at its heart the notion of sending and being sent.

MISLEADERSHIP: PAROCHIALISM AND HERESY

The positive references to 'the nations' in parts of Isaiah, and the call on Israel to be 'a light for the Gentiles' (Isaiah 42:6), were all very well in times of stability and peace, but as conditions deteriorated, and especially when faced with persecution and oppression, it is hardly surprising that Jewish attitudes towards the other nations began to harden.[7] The Essene community at Qumran, for example (largely known to us through the groundbreaking discovery of the Dead Sea Scrolls in the middle of the 20th century) took such teaching to an extreme.[8] The present world, they believed, was radically evil and doomed to destruction. The Essenes' calling was therefore to separate from the world, to keep themselves pure as a holy remnant and to wait for God's intervention. Most of their fellow Jews, these Essenes believed, were 'sons of darkness'—including devout Jews as well as those whom the Pharisees referred to as 'sinners' and Jesus as 'the lost'. The Essenes alone were the 'sons of light'. 'In such a climate', writes Bosch, 'even the idea of a missionary attitude to the Gentiles would be preposterous.'[9]

The Essenes' theology may have been cosmic in its scope but the practice of their faith was therefore parochial—limited to a group of consenting adults who lived in the desert and made strenuous efforts to avoid unnecessary contact with outsiders. It is unlikely that Jesus was thinking of this group in particular when he sat on a Galilean mountainside and began to teach the crowds about the kingdom of heaven, but his words clearly cut across such parochialism in all its forms:

You are the salt of the earth. But if the salt loses its saltiness, how can it be made salty again? … You are the light of the world. A city on a hill cannot be hidden. Neither do people light a lamp and put it under a bowl. Instead they put it on its stand, and it gives light to everyone in the house. In the same way, let your light shine before others, that they may see your good deeds and glorify your Father in heaven. (Matthew 5:13–16)

There is, however, a potentially more damaging alternative to an inward-looking parochialism, and that is a faith which is zealously promoted while remaining essentially toxic in its content. The poison may, on occasions, be of an antinomian nature—encouraging people to disregard the law altogether, to live life free from the shackles of any guiding moral principles—and we find many traces of this toxin in the New Testament, most notably among the Corinthians, to whom Paul writes despairingly, 'It is actually reported that there is sexual immorality among you, and of a kind that even pagans do not tolerate: a man has his father's wife. And you are proud!' (1 Corinthians 5:1). Yet the other extreme—a crusading legalism—is equally poisonous and also emerges regularly in the Gospels and thereafter.

The Pharisees in Jesus' day had a missionary arm, which enthusiastically promoted the virtues of their way of life to fellow Jews and even to Gentiles. There were two types of Gentile converts —described by the words 'God-fearer' and 'proselyte'—and both were to be found in some profusion, frequently listening to and joining in with the worship of the local synagogue.[10] 'God-fearing' Gentiles accepted the idea of one God and sought to live by the moral but not the ceremonial Jewish law. 'Proselytes', by contrast, accepted the ceremonial law and were circumcised, often becoming the most fanatical devotees of their new religion. The main aim of the pharisaical missionaries was to turn God-fearers into proselytes —a goal that was achieved in the case of Izates, the king of Adiabene (in modern-day Iraq), who became a God-fearer through the ministry of a Jew called Ananias but was then persuaded to 'go the whole way' (much to his mother's distress) through a Galilean evangelist named Eleazar.[11]

'Woe to you, teachers of the law and Pharisees, you hypocrites!' said Jesus in Matthew 23, referring to this movement within Pharisaism. 'You travel over land and sea to win a single convert, and then you make that convert twice as much a child of hell as you are' (v. 15)—this latter phrase perhaps acknowledging the tendency for the student to be more extreme than the teacher. It's a brief but devastating critique of a missionary movement that seems to have enjoyed its heyday during Jesus' own lifetime, and its inclusion within Matthew's Gospel may also be significant, given the ongoing and deeply regrettable tensions between the synagogue and the early Church, which found expression, around AD85, in the words of the Twelfth Benediction: 'Let the Nazarenes and the heretics be destroyed in a moment... Let their names be expurgated from the Book of Life and not be entered with those of the just.'[12]

Within the rest of the New Testament, we see examples of a similarly misplaced missionary zeal in action, most notably in Saul's attempts to nip the Christian 'heresy' in the bud. 'I was advancing in Judaism beyond many of my own age among my people,' he says in Galatians 1:14, 'and was extremely zealous for the traditions of my fathers'—a zeal clearly demonstrated in his persecution of the early church (see Philippians 3:6). Ironically, it was the same Saul, now renamed Paul, who had to contend with other 'zealots'— messianic cousins, as it were, of Eleazar the Galilean—who were pushing for the Gentile Christians to accept circumcision and the ceremonial law. 'These people are zealous to win you over,' Paul continued in Galatians 4, 'but for no good. What they want is to alienate you from us, so that you may have zeal for them. It is fine to be zealous, provided the purpose is good' (vv. 17–18).

This particular controversy came to a head in the Council of Jerusalem, where, according to Luke's account in Acts 15:1–35, a godly compromise was reached—a development that was essential for the future of the Church as a worldwide mission movement rather than another Jewish sect. Yet misplaced missionary zeal, even where unaccompanied by the physical violence of the 'Sicarii', the suicide bombers of their day,[13] remains a potent force for harm. Indeed,Paul's words to the Galatian believers are an excellent motto for every Christian believer: 'It is fine to be zealous, provided the purpose is good'.

As a footnote, it is interesting to find that both Jesus and Paul were decidedly uninterested in the motivation of the evangelists of their day. In Mark 9, the disciple John told Jesus that he 'saw someone driving out demons in your name and we told him to stop, because he was not one of us'. 'Do not stop him,' Jesus replied, '...for whoever is not against us is for us' (vv. 38–40). In Philippians 1, Paul wrote, 'Some preach Christ out of envy and rivalry, but others out of goodwill... But what does it matter? The important thing is that in every way, whether from false motives or true, Christ is preached. And because of this I rejoice' (vv. 15, 18).

In our postmodern world, there is a tendency to place sincerity (motivation) above truth (the message). Yet while good motivation has its place within Christian discipleship, the key issue in the early Church was the message itself—a gospel message that was supremely life-giving in contrast to both the bogus freedom of the antinomians and the oppressive legalism of the scribes and Pharisees. We might imagine a sick person saying, 'Is the doctor sincere?' In one sense the question doesn't matter very much, or at least it pales into insignificance when set alongside another question: 'Does the medicine work?'

JESUS OUR LORD

The shepherd, the 'pioneer and perfecter', the farmer: each has provided a potent model for different aspects of Jesus' leadership, but the image that best picks up the theme of 'Go for me' leadership is that of Jesus our Lord. For missionary leadership—the leadership that stands beside us with one hand on our shoulders, indicating with the other hand the direction in which we are to go—is supremely commanding. Only those who acknowledge Jesus as Lord will be willing to 'go' at his behest, especially if they do not have the reassuring sight of Jesus the pioneer going before them.

Jesus' 'Go for me' parables pick up this lordly theme, most often in reference to God himself (see Matthew 9:38; 21:33–44;

22:1–14). God is the 'Lord of the harvest', the landlord, the king. He variously sends out workers into his harvest field, servants (then his son) to collect the rent, and heralds bearing wedding invitations. No one presumes to disobey his orders, even though they end up beaten, stoned or dead. This is clearly authority of the highest order. There's a clarity and decisiveness about the whole enterprise that seems to brook no dissent.

The word 'Go!' on the lips of Jesus himself also occurs in the most commanding of contexts. Indeed, the most famous 'Go!' of them all is preceded by the words, 'All authority in heaven and on earth has been given to me' (Matthew 28:18). On earlier occasions, Jesus imposingly sent out the Twelve and the 72 with clear instructions about their mission to the Galilean villages (Luke 9:1; 10:1). In Matthew 23, he radically portrays himself as sending out 'prophets and sages and teachers' who will be pursued, flogged, crucified and killed (v. 34), although Luke's version of this saying, more traditionally, pictures God as the sender (11:49).

There can be no question, then, of either Jesus' authority or his missionary intentions. Both are abundantly clear from the moment he first called his disciples to 'fish for people' (Mark 1:17) and designated them apostles ('those who are sent'), so that 'they might be with him and that he might send them out to preach' (3:14). Such a start to his ministry could hardly be further from the inward-looking attitudes of his Qumran contemporaries.

There can be no question, either, that the message from the outset of Jesus mission was '*good* news': indeed, the very first verse of Mark's Gospel introduces us to 'the beginning of the good news about Jesus the Messiah'. The Pharisees could be zealous in their missionary endeavours but the result of their activities was bad news—oppressive, tiring, burdensome in the extreme. By contrast, in the famous 'Come to me' sayings, Jesus' yoke is easy and his burden light (Matthew 11:30).

The only question that might be raised concerns the breadth of Jesus' mission, which seems at first sight to encompass a remarkable range of people within the Jewish community, but with little to spare for those outside: 'I was sent only to the lost sheep of Israel,' as he put it succinctly to the Canaanite woman (Matthew 15:24). It's true that following Jesus' birth, the old man Simeon recognized him as 'a light for revelation to the Gentiles' (Luke 2:32).[14] After his death and resurrection, too, we read of a Jesus who commissions his followers to 'make disciples of all nations' (28:19) and to 'be my witnesses in Jerusalem, and in all Judea and Samaria, and to the ends of the earth' (Acts 1:8):[15] there can no question about the global nature of Jesus' mission at that point. Yet, as David Bosch demonstrates, these verses don't just come out of the blue. He asks, 'What is it that gave rise to the many sayings, parables and stories that seem, at the very least, to nourish the idea that, one day, God's covenant will reach far beyond the people of Israel? In my view,' he concludes, 'there can be no doubt: the primary inspiration for all these stories could only have been the provocative, boundary-breaking nature of Jesus' own ministry'.[16]

What, then, are the character qualities of the 'Go for me' leader? Missionary leadership in the Gospels requires decisiveness, discernment, vision and the somewhat elusive ability to comfort and reassure. It is these traits in the character of Jesus that have launched many thousands of missionary endeavours over the past two millennia, and it is to these qualities that we now turn.

THE CHARACTER OF OUR LORD

DECISIVENESS

The commanding nature of Jesus' call to 'Go!' and the clear instructions that he issued to the Twelve (and then the 72) suggest an unusual degree of decisiveness, to which the disciples instinctively responded. Indeed, decisiveness at its best—that winning combination of competence, urgency and clear communication—is enormously compelling in a world searching for purpose and direction.

In his contact with those whom the Pharisees branded as 'sinners', Jesus could urge individuals to take decisive action rather than allowing sinful situations to continue unchecked. 'Woman, where are they? Has no one condemned you?' he asked of the woman caught in adultery, in the little Gospel fragment preserved for us in John 8. 'No-one, sir,' she replied. 'Then neither do I condemn you' was the response. 'Go now and leave your life of sin' (vv. 10–11). The 'Go' in this case could be seen as a kind of pre-evangelism: a call to the woman to respond to her remarkable reprieve by repenting of her adulterous liaison and (if she were the married party) by returning to her husband.

In his contact with seekers—those who wished to follow him—Jesus could be equally decisive. In Mark 10 we are introduced to a man who seemed to have everything: he was young, rich, powerful, a person of integrity—every canny father's dream for a potential son-in-law. Outside John's Gospel, this young man is the only individual of whom it is written that Jesus 'loved him' (Mark 10:21). (In John 11:5 and 19:26, this accolade is awarded to Mary, Martha,

Lazarus and the apostle John.) Yet the call to 'Go' on this occasion was highly challenging: 'Go, sell everything you have and give to the poor, and you will have treasure in heaven. Then come, follow me' (v. 21). It cut right at the root of the man's security, his 'great wealth', and resulted in his quiet exit from the scene—never, it seems, to return.

Perhaps what's most surprising about the story is the way Jesus left it at that rather than entering into lengthy negotiations to get the man on board. He was swayed neither by his personal feelings of love nor by the obvious advantage of having such a powerful and wealthy individual on the team. No, Mammon was clearly both a false god and an addiction for this man, and there could be no compromise with the missionary call to go and take decisive action. Sometimes, as on this occasion, the toughness of the challenge of God can lead to sadness in both the caller and the called.

It was not just 'sinners' or seekers who heard this decisive call. In his discipleship teaching Jesus could be equally clear of the need to 'go' in cases where believers had fallen out with one another. In the Sermon on the Mount, he taught, 'If you are offering your gift at the altar and there remember that your brother or sister has something against you, leave your gift there in front of the altar. First go and be reconciled to that person; then come and offer your gift' (Matthew 5:23–24). Unresolved relationships can do untold damage in any family and are equally debilitating to the health and missionary calling of the family of God. Jesus was clear of the need to resolve those relationships rather than blithely carrying on with 'business as usual' in the temple. There is, after all, a human tendency—which Jesus here confronts—to put off the challenge of reconciliation by resorting to familiar rituals or 'comfort-food' religion—a further example of Bonhoeffer's 'cheap grace', which we focused on in Chapter 8.

'Go and sort out your lifestyle! Go and sort out your priorities! Go and sort out your relationships!' These challenges (perhaps couched in more pastorally sensitive language) will be familiar to every Christian leader committed to the vision of 'speaking the truth in love' (Ephesians 4:15). It takes real courage to present such challenges, for when we say 'Go!' we run the risk that people will never return—a risk that was clearly realized with the man whom Jesus loved.

Yet the alternative course of indecision and non-confrontation proves highly costly in the long term, to those who are led as much as to their leader. Situations remain unresolved for months or years; sinful patterns of behaviour remain unchallenged; marriages and team relationships slowly fall apart, or explode into a thousand jagged fragments. In some church communities (as a friend once put it) there is so much metaphorical dust swept under the carpet that the carpet lies three foot off the ground!

'Go!' said Jesus to the adulterous woman, the rich man and the gift-bearing brother at the altar, and there are situations where the wise leader will do the same. We can listen and counsel and support and pray but, ultimately, 'Go for me' leadership recognizes the dignity of those we lead and stresses their responsibility to make their own decisions and live their own lives under God's direction.

DISCERNMENT

Closely related to decisiveness, and to the insight of the 'Follow me' leader, 'Go for me' leadership at its best is discerning leadership. At its heart is not simply the fulfilment of the leader's vision but also the well-being and personal development of those charged with carrying the vision forward. In particular, there can be a danger of dependency—an over-reliance on an organization or its leadership —resulting in immaturity and stunted growth. In such situations, the command to 'Go!' may seem tough and uncompromising; yet no other approach will encourage people to take the initiative and stand on their own two feet.

There is an unusual incident in Mark's Gospel involving Jesus, a wild demonized man who calls himself 'Legion' and a whole herd of pigs. At the end of the story, there is a brief scene in which Mark writes, 'As Jesus was getting into the boat, the man who had been demon-possessed begged to go with him. Jesus did not let him, but said, "Go home to your own people and tell them how much the Lord has done for you"' (5:18–19).

Here was a man who plainly wanted to follow Jesus but was deliberately told to go. It's true that he was sent away to be a missionary to his family and village (a community that had lived in fear of this bogeyman, who no doubt played a part in many a young villager's nightmares), but the passion with which he begged to go with Jesus, and the simple phrase 'Jesus did not let him', still make for uncomfortable reading, especially given the man's vulnerability, having just experienced such a traumatic spiritual rebirth.

Reading between the lines, though, it becomes clear that Jesus was acting entirely in the man's best interests. In Legion he saw the victim of a regular cycle of abuse, hatred, violence and dependence on the demons who were driving him—the dependence of the addict, which both seduces and destroys. In Legion he also saw someone who had just been dramatically released from such degradation and whose unhealthy dependence on the demons could all too easily turn into an unhealthy dependence (in a different sense) on Jesus. Indeed, the man's begging in verse 18 has uncomfortable echoes of the begging earlier in the story, before the exorcism took place (vv. 10, 12).

And Jesus had the discernment to recognize that this man's needs would best be served by a call to a healthy independence (or, better still, interdependence), a call to change from victim to victor and to return to his community as the first evangelist to the east of the Sea of Galilee. Indeed, Legion's newfound dignity rested on a radical insight—that God has graciously made himself dependent on us, not simply us on him.[1]

Jesus' gamble certainly paid off. A little later he returned to the same district (the region of the Decapolis: Mark 7:31), where he might have expected to meet some suspicion after the loss of the pigs (5:17). Instead, he was given a warm welcome, and the reason for that change of heart is obvious: Legion had taken his newfound dignity as a 'fellow worker with God' extremely seriously, replacing his former role as the stuff of nightmares with his new role as witness and missionary, '[telling] in the Decapolis how much Jesus had done for him' (5:20).

It's a peculiar Gospel story, yet it gives us fresh insight into the need for 'Go for me' leadership. Long-term dependence on any individual or group will ultimately prove both demotivating and dehumanizing, reducing us to the condition of helpless children in a well-meaning 'nanny state'. Even dependence on Jesus himself needs to come under the theological spotlight, whatever its senti-mental associations and pietistic credentials. True, we are to depend on Jesus—he is the vine and we are the branches and, as he said to his disciples, 'apart from me you can do nothing' (John 15:5)—but he also graciously depends on us. It is the branches, after all, that bear fruit. Thus he rescues us from an impoverished vision of ourselves as victims, not victors; passive beneficiaries, not active contributors.

VISION

So we come to the heart of 'Go for me' leadership—our missionary calling to step out in faith, preach the gospel, heal the sick, feed the hungry, release the captives and encourage others to do the same.

In Luke's Gospel, Jesus' first mission trip was taken on his own. Having first set out his powerful manifesto in the synagogue in Nazareth, having moved from Nazareth to Capernaum by the lakeside, where he performed a number of miracles and exorcisms (including the healing of Simon's mother-in-law), Jesus next told the eager crowds who surrounded him, 'I must proclaim the good news of the kingdom of God to the other towns also, because that is why I was sent' (4:43). And as he went round preaching, he started noticing fishermen, tax collectors, revolutionaries, and began to assemble a group of disciples around him, whom he then designated apostles (6:13).

A couple of chapters later, we witness the second stage of what is beginning to resemble a training programme. Once again we see Jesus travelling about 'from one town and village to another, proclaiming the good news of the kingdom of God', but this time, we read, 'The Twelve were with him, and also some women' (8:1–2). The women contributed something to the mission trip: we are told that they were 'helping to support them out of their own means' (v. 3). The men don't seem to have contributed anything beyond the fact that they were simply 'with him', witnessing his miracles and seeking to grasp hold of his teaching.

The obvious third stage was to send out the disciples to do the kingdom work themselves, and that mission forms the theme of the early part of Luke 9. Here the apostles were given 'power and authority to drive out all demons and to cure diseases' (v. 1), then sent out two by two, according to Mark 6:7–9, with nothing but the clothes they stood up in.

At stage four, the apostles were joined by a larger group—72 of them in all—and Jesus sent them out with the same mission imperative. On their return, Luke tells us, these fledgling missionaries were full of it: 'The seventy-two returned with joy and said, 'Lord, even the demons submit to us in your name!' (10:17). Jesus too was completely delighted, as the joyful lyricism of his subsequent prayer demonstrates (vv. 21–22; Matthew 11:25–28). And for those attuned to the cadences of Luke, the combination of the Holy Spirit and the outpouring of joy that Jesus experienced on this occasion marks a significant stage in the progress of his mission. Jesus' birth, the return of the 72, the first Easter, the day of Pentecost, the conversion of Cornelius (which signified the true inauguration of the mission to the Gentiles): each of these events forms a marker-stone in Luke–Acts, and each is accompanied with an outpouring of joy and the Holy Spirit.[2]

And so to the final commissioning, and the farthest-reaching 'Go' of them all: in Acts 1:8, 'You will receive power when the Holy Spirit comes on you; and you will be my witnesses in Jerusalem, and in all Judea and Samaria, and to the ends of the earth'; in Matthew 28:19–29, 'Go and make disciples of all nations, baptizing them in the name of the Father and of the Son and of the Holy Spirit, and teaching them to obey everything I have commanded you (28:19–20); in a rather late addition to the gospel of Mark, 'Go into all the world and preach the gospel to all creation' (16:15). And then Jesus himself goes—returning to his Father's side.[3]

A childhood image comes to my mind: a picture of my father building sandcastles on the beach, with long walls, impressive towers and a moat running round the perimeter. He is not building sandcastles simply as a way of keeping us entertained. He's building them because he enjoys building them—and that joy is infectious, so that before long we children are joining in. Nearly 40 years on, we have grown into two university professors, a vicar and a social worker, with nine children of our own between us. Those nine have duly witnessed the joy of their parents building sandcastles and have caught the bug as well, so that a generation from now, there may be 20 sandcastle builders, then 50, then 100.

And something of that dynamic lies at the heart of Jesus' missionary vision, which starts from his own commitment as the first apostle, 'because that is why I was sent' (Luke 4:43), and quickly catches hold of others who share their lives with him. First twelve caught it, then 72, then 120, 3000, 5000 (Luke 6:13; 10:1; Acts 1:15; 2:41; 4:4): Luke has no qualms about charting the numerical growth of the whole enterprise. And so began the fulfilment of what must have seemed an impossibly daunting challenge to the first believers—the call to go into all the world and make disciples.

COMFORT

The English word 'comfort' is derived from the Latin phrase *con fortis* and means literally 'with strength'. In a well-known section of the Bayeux Tapestry, Bishop Odo (the brother of William the Conqueror) is seen poking his soldiers forward with a large spear-like stick, and above him is the Latin inscription, 'This is Bishop Odo comforting his troops'.

While such a definition (and, indeed, such provocation on Odo's part) might be seen to illustrate 'muscular Christianity' at its worst, sources of genuine comfort can sometimes be a little surprising. It's not that many people draw strength from an episcopal poke in the ribs, but a healthy realism that acknowledges both the greatness of the task and the dangers that lie ahead can prevent the onset of a paralysing disillusionment when those dangers duly arise, and can thus act as a spur for decisive action. Moving from 1066 through to the dark days of 1940, there is no question that Winston Churchill's first speech on becoming Prime Minister proved highly inspirational. Here, if ever, we see a man 'comforting his troops':

We have before us an ordeal of the most grievous kind. We have before us many, many long months of struggle and of suffering. You ask, what is our policy? I can say: it is to wage war, by sea, land and air, with all our might and with all the strength that God can give us; to wage war against a monstrous tyranny, never surpassed in the dark, lamentable catalogue of human crime. That is our policy. You ask, what is our aim? I can answer in one word: it is victory, victory at all costs, victory in spite of all terror; victory, however long and hard the road may be; for without victory, there is no survival. [4]

In Jesus, of course, we see the missionary call accompanied by more conventional expressions of comfort. In Luke 10, for example, he received news of the successful mission trip of the 72 and shared in their joy—an excellent example of the encouraging debrief. In

Matthew 28 he accompanied the challenge of the Great Commission with a promise that 'surely I am with you always, to the very end of the age' (v. 20), and in John's Gospel that promise was fleshed out further in his teaching on the Holy Spirit—'another Comforter' who would be with them for ever (14:16, KJV). Both the gentle reception of the Spirit in John 20, where Jesus quietly breathed on his disciples, and the noisy reception of the Spirit in Acts 2, complete with violent wind and tongues of flame, provided just the strength the Church needed to begin to fulfil its mission.

Yet there is also a realism about the task that lies ahead, which provides comfort of a more Churchillian kind: 'Go! I am sending you out like lambs among wolves,' Jesus told the disciples (Luke 10:3), and then 'Be on your guard; you will be handed over to the local councils and be flogged in the synagogues... Everyone will hate you because of me, but those who stand firm to the end will be saved' (Matthew 10:17, 22).

Muscular Christianity? Most certainly. For spiritual flabbiness is hardly the defining mark of those sent out by Jesus.

✠

JESUS' CALLING FROM THE FATHER

In his poem 'The Coming', R.S. Thomas pictures God holding a small globe in his hand and pointing to a 'scorched land of fierce colour', through which a river flows, a 'bright serpent… radiant with slime'. In this fallen Eden a bare tree stands on a bare hill, and many people stretch out their hands towards it, 'as though waiting for a vanished April'. The Son of God watches on, and then responds to his Father's unasked question: 'Let me go there.'

Thomas' poem beautifully expresses the willingness of the Son to embrace his missionary call—a willingness expressed, too, in Philippians 2, probably the oldest Christian hymn recorded for us:

> *Your attitude should be the same as that of Christ Jesus:*
> *Who, being in very nature God,*
> *did not consider equality with God something to be grasped,*
> *but made himself nothing,*
> *taking the very nature of a servant,*
> *being made in human likeness.*
> *And being found in appearance as a man,*
> *he humbled himself*
> *and became obedient to death—*
> *even death on a cross (vv. 5–8, NIV).*

In both the modern poem and the ancient hymn, the implication is the same: Jesus volunteered for the task. There is no question of the Son having his arm twisted by a desperate Father, no sense that the Son had to say, 'I'll need to go away and think about it.' Instead, like Isaiah the prophet, we are called to envisage a heavenly consultation at which the question is being asked, 'Whom shall I send? And who will go for us?' and Jesus steps forward to respond: 'Here am I. Send me' (see Isaiah 6:8).

The hymn in Philippians ends with that great vision of Jesus being 'exalted... to the highest place' and given 'the name that is above every name, that at the name of Jesus every knee should bow, in heaven and on earth and under the earth, and every tongue confess that Jesus Christ is Lord, to the glory of God the Father' (vv. 9–11, NIV).

It is Jesus' willing acceptance of the call of God, in other words, that gives him the ultimate authority as 'Lord', as the caller and sender of others. In the Gospels, we see that Lordship at work, as Jesus has authority to send out apostles, prophets, sages and teachers (Matthew 28:18–19; 23:34), alongside evil spirits (8:31–32), angels (Mark 13:27) and even, it appears, the Holy Spirit himself.[1] And what is the source of that Lordship? In a succinct phrase in John 20:21: 'As the Father has sent me, I am sending you.'

'As the Father has sent me': it's an idea that appears on numerous occasions in John's Gospel, where 'the Father' and 'him who sent me' seem to be used almost interchangeably as descriptions of God. In the other Gospels, too, Jesus' understanding that he has been 'sent' provides the backdrop to some of his key mission statements: 'I was sent only to the lost sheep of Israel' (Matthew 15:24); 'I must proclaim the good news... to the other towns also, because that is why I was sent' (Luke 4:43); and, in the Nazareth synagogue, 'The Spirit of the Lord is on me, because he has anointed me to proclaim good news to the poor. He has sent me to proclaim freedom for the prisoners and recovery of sight for the blind, to set the oppressed free, to proclaim the year of the Lord's favour' (4:18–19, quoting Isaiah 61:1–2).

One of the few phrases that is shared by all four Gospels links Jesus' sense of being sent with the reception that his own apostles will be given: 'Anyone who welcomes you welcomes me, and whoever welcomes me welcomes the one who sent me' (Matthew

10:40).[2] Another of Jesus' great mission statements—his call 'not...
to be served, but to serve, and to give his life as a ransom for many'
(Mark 10:45) is paralleled by Paul in Romans 8:3: 'For what the law
was powerless to do... God did by sending his own Son in the
likeness of sinful humanity to be a sin offering.'

There are various Greek words translated 'send' in these and
related passages, but by far the most common is the verb *apostello*,
with its connotations of sending forth, sending with a commission.
This word is used most movingly of all in Jesus' parable of the
tenants in the vineyard, where we read of the landlord, 'He had one
left to send, a son, whom he loved. He sent him last of all, saying,
"They will respect my son." But the tenants said to one another,
"... Let's kill him"' (Mark 12:6–7).

'A son, whom he loved': in this phrase Jesus picked up on the
words he had heard at his baptism: 'You are my Son, whom I love'
(Mark 1:11). Just as Winston Churchill 'comforted' his nation with
a vision of 'blood, toil, tears and sweat', so Jesus, in the teeth of
growing persecution, was 'comforted' by the knowledge that his
own baptismal calling—the reason he was sent—was not simply to
be a beloved Son. It was rather to be a beloved Son who would give
his life as a ransom for many.

Previous references to Jesus as the primary apostle are therefore
not fanciful, but instead lie at the heart of the Gospel witness, in
which Jesus has a clear sense of having been made an apostle by
his Father. The disciples were called apostles because Jesus was
apostolic first—or, perhaps, to take the image further still, 'In
Christ, God was his own apostle'.[3]

What, then, was Jesus sent to do? To those, like myself, who are
somewhat suspicious of the easy soundbite, the pithy one-liner that
summarizes complex truth in a single phrase, it's encouraging to
note the variety of Jesus' mission statements, which include words
like 'kingdom', 'proclaim', 'seek', 'save', 'good news' and 'ransom'
but never seek to bring them all together into one grand composite
whole. What started as an apparently local mission among the

Galilean hills and villages—a mission to the 'lost sheep of Israel'—was really global in its scope, as 'other sheep' would be gathered into the fold (John 10:16). Even Pontius Pilate seems, half unwittingly, to have discerned that there was some wider significance to Jesus' mission, and especially to its culmination at Golgotha. According to John's account, he 'had a notice prepared and fastened to the cross. It read, "JESUS OF NAZARETH, THE KING OF THE JEWS"... and the sign was written in Aramaic, Latin and Greek' (19:19–20).

While it might be difficult to construct a pithy 'mission statement' from the Gospel record, there remains a clear sense that Jesus knew both what he was called to do and, equally importantly, what he was not called to do. In fact, for many leaders, both Christian and otherwise, there is often as great a need for an 'unmission statement' as for its more positive alternative. Unlike some of the crusading Pharisees, Jesus himself was not called to 'travel over land and sea to win a single convert' (Matthew 23:15), although his apostles would be sent to do precisely that. Unlike the various messianic pretenders of his day, Jesus was not called to raise an army against Roman oppression. Unlike Paul, the 'apostle to the Gentiles', Jesus was not called to strategic mission work outside the Jewish community. The story of the temptations in the wilderness is far more a story of what Jesus was not called to do than a story in which his calling itself was clearly formulated. And for all who seek God's calling on their lives, an initial sense of their 'uncalling' may well begin to guide them along the right track.

Returning to Jesus' call, there is one image in the Exodus story that provides an archetype for his sense of being 'sent' by the Father—the burning bush. Just as Moses had been called to 'come to me' in the tent of meeting, to 'follow me' in the pillars of cloud and fire, and to 'wait for me' in the desert, so it was in his very first encounter with the divine—in the flames of fire on Horeb, the mountain of God—that Moses was called to 'Go for me'.

The story is well known (Exodus 3:1—4:17). Moses, an exile in the land of Midian, was tending his father-in-law's sheep when he was arrested by a strange phenomenon: a bush that appeared to be on fire but was not burning up. On approaching the bush, he was called by name, then told to take off his sandals 'for the place where you are standing is holy ground' (3:5). God introduced himself to the frightened shepherd as 'the God of your father, the God of Abraham, the God of Isaac and the God of Jacob' (v. 6), then spoke powerfully of his compassion for his people in the face of their oppression at the hands of the Egyptians. 'I have come down to rescue them…' said the Lord, 'and to bring them up out of that land into a good and spacious land, a land flowing with milk and honey' (v. 8).

Lest that should sound too easy—too triumphalistic, perhaps—the Lord continued with a word of Churchillian 'comfort', for this land 'flowing with milk and honey' was also 'the home of the Canaanites, Hittites, Amorites, Perizzites, Hivites and Jebusites' (v. 8)—a simple fact that would eventually result in 'blood, toil, tears and sweat' to a quite alarming degree. And so to the crunch moment: 'So now, go. I am sending you to Pharaoh to bring my people the Israelites out of Egypt' (v. 10)—a command that was met with a series of objections on Moses' part, some genuine, others contrived, to which God responded with the utmost seriousness.

At first sight, there seems little correlation between this story and the call of Jesus. The nearest equivalent in the Gospels are the two great revelatory moments of Jesus' baptism and his transfiguration, but the disparity between these accounts and the story of the burning bush could hardly be more clear.

For one thing, Jesus received no clear divine commission at these pivotal moments: on both occasions he simply heard the words, 'This is my Son, whom I love; with him I am well pleased' (Matthew 3:17; 17:5). For another, the focus of attention was not on an external phenomenon through which the glory of God was revealed: it was rather on Jesus, who appeared himself as the revelation of God's glory. Nor could there be a greater contrast between the reluctance of Moses and the willingness of Jesus to respond to God's call.

On closer inspection, however, the burning bush and the transfiguration do bear some striking similarities—not simply in the juxtaposition of fire, mountains and the presence of God, which links Moses the law-giver, Elijah the prophet and Jesus the Messiah, but also in the nature of the callings themselves.

At the burning bush, Moses is given an awesome vision of the God who is—'I Am Who I Am' (Exodus 3:14), the origin of the 'tetragrammaton', the Hebrew name for God, variously translated 'Yahweh', 'Jehovah' or the LORD in capital letters. Yet the God who is proves to be in the business of doing as well as being. The Lord of the burning bush is an 'apostolic' God who is planning a glorious rescue mission on behalf of his oppressed people—an exodus in which Moses is to be equipped and sent out to play a pivotal role.

On the mount of transfiguration, the disciples are given a similar revelation, and, while Moses 'hid his face because he was afraid to look at God' (v. 6), the disciples 'fell face down to the ground, terrified' in the presence of the transfigured Jesus (Matthew 17:6). This Jesus who is—this 'Son whom I love'—is perfectly in tune with the apostolic heart of his Father. But the disciples' mission is to be an even more significant rescue operation, taking on the full might not of the 'Canaanites, Hittites, Amorites, Perizzites, Hivites and Jebusites', but rather of 'the rulers... the authorities... the powers of this dark world and... the spiritual forces of evil in the heavenly realms' (Ephesians 6:12). There is no question about the crucial nature of this ultimate apostolic mission, or about the blood, toil, tears and sweat required for its fulfilment.

The point is drawn out especially clearly by Luke in his account of this mountain-top experience, for as Moses and Elijah appeared alongside Jesus, 'they spoke about his departure, which he was about to bring to fulfilment at Jerusalem' (9:31). The word for 'departure' here is a somewhat unusual one. Luke could easily have used the far more common Greek word *thanatos* if he had wanted simply to refer to Jesus' death, but instead he uses the word *exodos*. It's a detail all too easily missed in English versions, which usually translate the word as 'decease', 'death' or 'departure',[4] but the implication is clear. As Tom Wright puts it, 'In the first Exodus, Moses led the Israelites out of slavery in Egypt and home to the promised land. In the new Exodus, Jesus will lead all God's people out of their slavery of sin and death, and home to their promised inheritance—the new creation in which the whole world will be redeemed.'[5]

'Go for me': on the lips of the beloved Son, who has been given all authority, the command sounds reasonable enough. If Jesus our Lord calls us to go, we should go, just as Jesus himself perfectly fulfilled the divine commission of his Father.

But what about normal, fallible human leadership? Such leaders might have the winsomeness to call on others to 'come to me', the integrity to challenge others to 'follow me' and the wisdom to invite others to 'wait for me'. Yet is 'Go for me' one step too far in terms of human authority? And if not, what are the preconditions for godly 'Go for me' leadership?

RESPONDING TO THE MISSIONARY CHALLENGE

Dr Kiran Martin is a remarkable woman. Shortly after completing a postgraduate diploma in Paediatrics, she became aware of a cholera epidemic in Ambedkar Basti, one of the slums on the outskirts of Delhi, and was determined to help. There were very few resources available so Dr Martin began to treat patients at a borrowed table under a tree outside the slum, and from there she started to visit the slum dwellers, wading through the mud and rubbish that had built up in the narrow spaces between their makeshift houses.

From those small beginnings, Dr Martin founded Asha,[1] a community health and development society currently working in 45 slums around Delhi, changing the lives of their inhabitants beyond recognition. As part of the strategy, many hundreds of slum dwellers, almost all women, have been trained as Community Health Visitors (or 'Barefoot Doctors', as they are known) and Lane Volunteers, looking after the basic health and social needs of their area. Witnessing the work at first hand on a recent mission trip, it was a great privilege to meet many of these women, to listen to their stories, work together, laugh together and pray together.

And reflecting on that experience a few months on, the secret of Asha's success seems clear. Just as the early Church had a dynamic of multiplication that amazed the likes of Pliny and Suetonius, so multiplication—the 'Go for me' dynamic—lies at the heart of Kiran Martin's vision, frequently causing equal astonishment in Delhi's corridors of power.[2] The cholera epidemic in Ambedkar Basti provided the catalyst for Dr Martin, a thoughtful and deeply committed

Christian, to discover her lifetime's calling—a growing sense that God was sending her to bring hope and healing to some of the poorest communities in the world. Nearly 20 years later, this 'apostle' is sending out hundreds of further 'apostles' to continue the work, many of whom have come to a living faith in the process—so that Asha's ministry currently touches the lives of more than a quarter of a million people.

'As the Father has sent me, I am sending you' (John 20:21). It's a missionary dynamic that has continued to motivate and inspire the Church from its earliest days to our own. In the book of Acts we read of Saul's 'burning bush' experience on the road to Damascus (9:1–18):[3] an encounter with the risen Christ before whom he, like Moses before him, fell to the ground in astonishment and fear. 'Moses, Moses,' came the voice from the burning bush. 'Saul, Saul,' came the voice from heaven, and then came the commission itself, as recorded in Paul's later defence before King Agrippa:

'I have appeared to you to appoint you as a servant and a witness of what you have seen of me and what I will show you. I will rescue you from your own people and from the Gentiles. I am sending [apostello] you to them, to open their eyes and turn them from darkness to light, and from the power of Satan to God, so that they may receive forgiveness of sins, and a place among those who are sanctified by faith in me.' (Acts 26:16–18, NIV)

Whether that commission was given directly by Jesus or via the understandably nervous disciple Ananias is not entirely clear, but there is no question of Paul's sense of calling—of apostleship—from that moment on. That calling was primarily to be a ministry of teaching and evangelism, increasingly focused on Gentiles, both pagan and God-fearing, so that Paul could later write to the church in Corinth, 'Unlike so many, we do not peddle the word of God for profit. On the contrary, in Christ we speak before God with sincerity, as those sent from God' (2 Corinthians 2:17). Paul could be equally clear of his 'uncalling', too: as he wrote in an earlier letter to

Corinth, 'Christ did not send me to baptize, but to preach the gospel' (1 Corinthians 1:17). Paul's was not, we might infer, the settled ministry of the pastor but the pioneering ministry of the evangelist.

The risen Christ may have used his servant Ananias to give Paul his marching orders, but elsewhere in the book of Acts it is frequently the church that does the sending. The church in Jerusalem, we're told, 'sent Barnabas to Antioch' to see what was going on in that exciting and vibrant fellowship (11:22); the church in Antioch, led by the Holy Spirit, later 'placed their hands' on Saul and Barnabas and 'sent them off' on Paul's first missionary journey (13:3). When the pair returned to Antioch, the church then 'sent them on their way' again (15:3), this time to represent the fellowship at the crucial Council of Jerusalem, and later in that chapter the Jerusalem church sent Paul and Barnabas back to Antioch, along with two of their own number, Judas and Silas (v. 22).

Paul could also do the sending himself. He showed decisiveness as a 'Go for me' leader in sending Titus and 'our brother' (most probably Luke) to sort out the mess in Corinth (2 Corinthians 12:18). He demonstrated genuine pastoral discernment in his decision to persuade Onesimus, the runaway slave, to return to his master Philemon, 'no longer as a slave but... as a dear brother' (Philemon 16). His mentoring of the young Timothy, which included mission trips both with and without the apostle, illustrates Paul's visionary credentials, training up others to continue the work after him,[4] and the commissioning of the Ephesian elders in Acts 20 contains a fair dose of Churchillian comfort, similar to that administered by Jesus himself: 'I know that after I leave, savage wolves will come in among you and will not spare the flock... So be on your guard' (vv. 29, 31); then, more positively, 'Now I commit you to God and to the word of his grace, which can build you up and give you an inheritance among all those who are sanctified' (v. 32).

The loyalty of these people to the apostle and their recognition of his authority as a 'Go for me' leader are striking, especially given the frequently arduous nature of the tasks they were commissioned to do. Yet the depth of Paul's own sense of calling and the deeply sacrificial way in which that calling was lived out proved highly inspirational to others who encountered it. 'Go for me, as I go for Christ' might well have been his watchword, as this one missionary sent out hundreds of others.

SHEPHERDS AND FISHERMEN

Few Christians nowadays go to the lengths of the Essenes in their quest for a pure church. The caves of Qumran are now uninhabited and today's monastic communities tend to be generous and outward-looking in their orientation, rather than setting themselves over and against the 'sons of darkness' outside.

There is, however, an alarming parochialism that continues to pervade much of the church today, an unspoken mentality—in the British psyche, at least—that comes to regard the local church as a kind of club for like-minded members. It's not that anyone puts up a sign outside their church proclaiming, 'Only confident, white, middle-class heterosexual people without any problems allowed here.' It's not that the apartheid is quite so explicit,[5] but people very quickly realize whether or not they are welcome in a place; whether they'll be listened to without a patronizing, superficial or moralistic response; whether they'll be welcomed as they are, without having to leave key parts of their identity or painful personal struggles at the church door. And the church's failure to engage at this level has frequently led to a pattern of communal life far removed from the outward-looking 'sociological impossibility' that so wrong-footed Pliny and his Roman contemporaries (see pages 138–139).

Few fellowships have the temerity to regard themselves as the 'One True Church', but the costly requirement for a fellowship to be both missionary and radically inclusive can all too easily be subverted by a desire for a quiet life and the 'comfort-food' religion that we mentioned earlier.

Such parochialism can infect Christian leaders, whether or not they work within the confines of a formal parish system. All too often, church leaders regard their task as pastoring a gathered community rather than 'putting out into deep water' to 'fish for people' (see Luke 5:4; Mark 1:17). It's not that the pastoral calling is unimportant, of course. Whatever pastoral structures the church leader sets up, there is no question that the sheep need care, nourishment, encouragement and guidance. But the missionary dynamic requires the leader to be 'putting out into deep water' on a regular basis. 'Go for me, as I go for Christ' only works where the leader has a vision that extends beyond the parochial, and when he or she is habitually to be found on or beyond the margins of the gathered community.[6]

There are many potential discouragements along this track. For one thing, the flock may not share the vision of their pastor and may resent the amount of time given over to missionary activities. 'She's not like the old vicar,' they mutter. 'He used to visit us every week.' For another, those on the margins (and beyond) may feel uncomfortable and challenged by the presence of a church leader among them, at least in the initial stages of the relationship. 'She's not like the old vicar', *they* mutter, 'He used to leave us alone!'

Even among colleagues, especially those whose own theology and practice tends towards parochialism, such missionary leadership is often regarded with considerable suspicion. Those called, for example, to plant new fellowships in areas where the church's witness is virtually non-existent frequently have to put up with the charge of triumphalism and empire-building, on top of the considerable sacrifice involved in sending out some of their most trusted and beloved fellow workers. Such an experience can be galling, to say the least.

Whatever the setbacks, however, it is clear that the credibility and effectiveness of 'Go for me' leadership depends, in very large part, on the vision and practice of the leaders themselves. Nor is there any question that a church without some form of 'Go for me' dynamic has an alarmingly limited shelf-life.

Parochialism is one thing; the zealous propagation of toxic teaching is quite another, but once again we cannot be complacent about the current state of the church in this regard, or the inherent 'rightness' of what it teaches.

It would be a caricature, bordering on the libellous, to portray the liberal wing of the Church as today's antinomians or the conservative wing as today's legalists. Almost every Christian, of whatever hue, would agree that we are saved by God's grace on the one hand and are called to be 'salt' and 'light' on the other. From the earliest days of the Church's mission, however, there has been both an antinomian and a legalistic tendency within its ranks, with both sides of the debate claiming divine authorization for their views, based on different aspects of the Gospel record. One group regards the other as unreconstructed Pharisees, while the other regards the first as unreconstructed pagans. 'It is fine to be zealous, provided the purpose is good,' wrote Paul (Galatians 4:18), yet, almost by definition, all zealots believe that 'the purpose is good', on whatever side of the divide they place themselves.

It is easy within this debate for each group to question the motivation of those with whom they disagree—in the heated exchanges over sexuality, for example, to suggest that the unreconstructed Pharisees are inherently homophobic and the unreconstructed pagans inherently immoral. In some cases, there may even be truth in such a charge. But both Jesus and Paul, as we have seen, appear relatively uninterested in the slippery question of motivation: on the evidence of the New Testament, this issue seems something of a sideshow. Their concern is rather to discover and propagate the truth—a quest that, for today's Church, will involve prayer, humility, painstaking study and costly obedience to whatever that truth may require of us.

It's at this point, though, that the thoughtful leader is faced with a tricky dilemma. How important are the issues that threaten to divide us? Are they really so significant as to deflect our attention away from our first calling to worship God and advance his kingdom? When Jesus sent his disciples out like heralds, inviting the people of his day to a great banquet, surely he wasn't expecting them to get tied up in knots over the precise wording of the invitation, its clauses and subclauses? Surely the very image itself seems to militate against the formulation of a hundred pages of carefully crafted small print?

There is another side to the argument, however, as our analysis of 'cheap grace' in Chapter 8 made clear. True, we are to 'go' to invite people to the most glorious of banquets, the most lavish of wedding receptions (Luke 14:16–24; Matthew 22:1–14), yet we are also to go to 'make disciples of all nations, baptizing them... and teaching them to obey everything I have commanded you' (Matthew 28:19–20). Carefully working out just what it is that Jesus commanded, most especially in those areas where his teaching is not explicit, is therefore an inescapable part of the Church's missionary calling, and cannot be lightly written off as insignificant or irrelevant. 'If anyone causes one of these little ones—those who believe in me—to stumble,' warns Jesus starkly, 'it would be better for them if a large millstone were hung round their neck and they were thrown into the sea' (Mark 9:42).

At first sight, this whole debate leaves us in the most difficult of situations, apparently paralysed in our missionary endeavours until the theologians and ethicists have agreed a common approach to the various dilemmas that confront us. We could, we suspect, be waiting a very long time. But there is great encouragement to be gleaned from the example of Jesus, of Paul, and of many others who proved themselves able to share the gospel with unbelievers while simultaneously engaging in passionate, frequently heated debate with their fellow believers. Paul's outrage at the incest taking place within the Corinthian church, for example (1 Corinthians 5)— incidentally, one of those very areas that Jesus himself never tackled explicitly—was entirely justified in view of the church's calling to be 'salt' and 'light'. Yet Paul never allowed that outrage to dominate his agenda or stop him from carrying out his primary calling as evangelist, church planter and 'apostle to the Gentiles'.

Parochialism and heresy both militate against the missionary call of the Church and both produce equally deadening results. When Jesus was challenged to explain the somewhat disreputable company who surrounded him, he responded, 'It is not the healthy who need a doctor, but those who are ill. I have not come to call the righteous, but sinners' (Mark 2:17). Had he been a truly parochial doctor, he would have had no patients—or, at least, no sick ones. Had he been a heretical doctor, his waiting list would have been full and so would his cupboards—full of quack remedies ranging from the useless to the downright dangerous.

And true 'Go for me' leadership—based on the Lordship of Christ—will always combine a passion for the welfare and blessing of the patient with an equal passion for the goodness and purity of the medicine.

THE BURNING BUSH

Jesus is Lord and we are not, so the final question of this section is an important one. On what basis can today's leaders call on their people to 'Go for me?' What gives us the kind of personal authority to send people out, especially on mission tasks whose inherent dangers and pitfalls we are called to spell out clearly and without embarrassment?

It's in the burning bush that we find something of an answer: a memory that must have resurfaced on many occasions as the sheer magnitude of Moses' calling became ever more apparent. For in the burning bush Moses encountered God—both a God who is ('I am who I am', Exodus 3:14) and a God who does ('I have come down to rescue them', v. 8). In the burning bush Moses also encountered himself—both a man who is ('Moses, Moses', v. 4) and a man called to do ('So now, go. I am sending you to Pharaoh to bring my people… out of Egypt', v. 10). There was an urgency to the task in hand—the very future of the Israelite nation was at stake—and

Moses' initial reaction to his commissioning, the series of excuses that take up the majority of Exodus 3—4, was not going to thwart the Lord's purposes. As Jesus later taught in a little parable, God is far more delighted by those who respond 'I will not' but later change their mind than by those who enthusiastically answer, 'I will, sir' but never bother to show up (Matthew 21:28–31).

The burning bush speaks of three fundamental factors that underlie the authority of today's 'Go for me' leader: first, a clear vision of God—who he is and what he plans to do; second, a clear vision of ourselves—who we are and what is our part in the fulfilment of those plans; and third, a sense of urgency in the task that lies ahead. Not everyone is called to an experience quite as dramatic as Moses' or as Paul's on the Damascus road: a lifetime's calling may come as we sit at a borrowed table under a tree, like Dr Kiran Martin, or as we browse through a newspaper or sit before an interview panel. But if we are to send out others, it is essential that we first know ourselves to be sent—that we have the ability both to understand and articulate our own sense of calling, the missionary task that has been entrusted to us.

The task of finding our calling (and, indeed, our 'uncalling') is not an entirely individual matter. As we have seen, Paul, among others, had the experience of being 'sent out' by the congregation at Antioch, even describing himself on one occasion as the 'servant' of the church (Colossians 1:25), and he in turn went on to send out others. But while our fellow believers may help to shape and refine our sense of calling, and perhaps to determine the context in which it is to be played out, this is not an area in which others should generally have the final word. The church in Antioch sent Paul and Barnabas on their way after hearing a prophecy at a dynamic prayer meeting (Acts 13:1–3); but Paul and Barnabas were present at the meeting too, and we can have little doubt that the prophetic word immediately resonated with their own sense of mission and calling as well as that of their fellow believers.

In his helpful book *Growing Leaders*, James Lawrence takes this thinking a step further in his encouragement for all Christian leaders to develop a 'personal life statement'—a description 'of where we think God is leading us', which 'helps provide focus, discernment and direction, like a compass guiding us through the maze of decisions about how to use our time, [and] pointing us to God's priorities for our life'.[7] Lawrence's is a highly pragmatic and accessible approach to what can seem a daunting and a somewhat subjective task, and the question with which his Chapter 5 opens demonstrates his awareness of the urgent need to discern our 'uncalling' too. 'There is enough time in the day to do everything God wants you to do,' he writes. 'So if you haven't got enough time, what needs to go?'

To return to our central theme, then, there is no question of the need for 'Go for me' leadership in the context of a world that is spiritually sick, deeply unjust and in desperate need of the life-giving medicine of the gospel in all its manifestations. In the West, in particular, where the Church's influence continues to decline, it is vital to rediscover that dynamic of multiplication, so that Pliny's experience of a 'great many individuals of every age and class, both men and women' might be replicated in our own day.

Missionary leaders will need to take risks—the risks that Jesus took in sending out twelve, then 72 inexperienced, even clueless, 'missioners' to bring in the kingdom of God. Missionary leaders will need to tell it as it is, to rediscover the brutal honesty of a Churchill, which is curiously comforting in the heat of the battle. But above all, missionary leaders will need to be doing it themselves—not sending out the troops by email from the comfort of a warm office but themselves responding daily to the urgent challenge of a missionary God who is and who does, who calls us each by name and assigns us a task that is completely beyond us; or would be were it not for 'his energy, which so powerfully works' within us (Colossians 1:29, NIV).

✣

Conclusion

LEADERS, FOLLOWERS AND THE CHARACTER OF JESUS

I first came across Chuck Lathrop's poetic parable 'In search of a Roundtable' some 20 years ago, and I remember being particularly struck by these lines:

> *It will take some sawing*
> *To be roundtabled,*
> *Some redefining*
> *And redesigning.*
> *Some redoing and rebirthing*
> *Of narrowlong Churching*
> *Can painful be*
> *For people and tables.*
> *It would mean no daising*
> *And throning,*
> *For but one king is there,*
> *And he was a footwasher*
> *At table no less.*[1]

It was partly, perhaps, that I had recently been worshipping in the Round Church—a beautiful Norman structure in the centre of Cambridge—and had noticed how later additions to the building had deliberately made its shape (and its worship) more conventional, complete with chancel and side aisles: a 'narrowlong' church, as Lathrop describes it. It was partly, too, that I had been brought up in Winchester, where a medieval round table adorns the wall of the Great Hall of the castle—not King Arthur's round table, sadly, but a medieval interpretation of the Arthurian myth, dating back to the 14th century.

Large round tables have their drawbacks, of course. The Winchester table is 18 feet in diameter, and it is hard to see how King Arthur's knights (or anyone else, for that matter) could have conducted easy conversation across such an expanse. Yet, as an image of the Church, and as a summary of the 'come', 'follow', 'wait' and 'go' of Christian leadership, it has much to commend it. The Church consists of men and women, young people and children, who are all called around the table as forgiven sinners, disciples and children of the King of kings. We come to that table to have fellowship with the king and with one another. We speak together of his words and deeds and urge each other to follow him wholeheartedly. We wait expectantly for his arrival, then celebrate his presence among us with joy and singing. And finally, in the words of dismissal that conclude the Eucharist, we 'go in peace to love and serve the Lord'—sent out to perform errands and fight battles (even, on occasions, to rescue damsels in distress) on his behalf and at his request.

Is there room for human leadership in the image of the round table? If so, it can only be as the first among equals—or perhaps as the last among equals, given the presence among us of the royal footwasher, the pioneer and perfecter of our faith. Some may be gifted with natural leadership qualities or even with a 'charisma' of leadership: in Romans 12, Paul encourages his readers to exercise whatever spiritual gifts they have, and (somewhere near the end of the list) instructs those with a gift of leadership to 'do it diligently' (v. 8).[2] Whatever the leadership charisma, though, our first calling is to remain as close as we can to the servant-king, to his presence, his integrity, his endurance and his missionary call.

The request of James and John, 'Let one of us sit at your right and the other at your left in your glory' (Mark 10:37) is not in itself unreasonable as we sit around this table. It is quite natural, even laudable, to wish to be placed in the near vicinity of our host. But it will invariably be met by the counter-question, 'Can you drink the cup I drink or be baptized with the baptism I am baptized with?' (v. 38). 'How far are we willing to model our lives on the call and character of Jesus?' is the nub of the issue, not 'How far can our leadership gifts be recognized and applauded?'

This table fellowship is, as we saw in Chapter 13, 'without analogy, indeed a sociological impossibility',[3]—far removed, in this regard, from its more monochrome Arthurian equivalent. It is a remarkably (sometimes disgracefully) diverse group of people from 'every tribe and language and people and nation', purchased with the blood of the Lamb and called to be 'a kingdom and priests to serve our God' (Revelation 5:9–10).

'COME, FOLLOW, WAIT, GO': SOME WIDER APPLICATIONS

The image of the round table has already suggested one new context in which the four leadership commands of Jesus are played out— the framework of the Eucharist. 'Come' and 'Go' take their natural places at the beginning and end of the service, while 'Follow' and 'Wait'—the call to obey Christ and receive him afresh through the bread and wine, and the infilling presence of the Holy Spirit— regularly renew the believer's desire to live life to God's praise and glory. For those charged with the responsibility of putting such services together, the challenge is clear: there is a constant need to attend to the warmth of our welcome, the relevance of our preaching, the prayerful expectation of our people and the missionary call with which the worship is concluded as we 'go in peace' to share in a kingdom ministry that is 'both mine and yours'.[4]

An act of worship that is cold and impersonal, unrelated to daily Christian living, rushed and parochially focused will seldom prove inspiring or motivating for its participants (although John 3:8 reminds us that 'the wind blows wherever it pleases', and in God's economy there are grace-filled exceptions to almost all such 'rules'). A service which, among its other virtues, allows space for both the people of God and the Spirit of God to breathe—'still space' rather than merely 'silent space', with that stillness pregnant with a sense of joyful expectancy[5]—is perhaps the closest we get to a fulfilment of the prayer, 'Your kingdom come… on earth as in heaven', especially where accompanied by the healing, reconciling love and power that are the hallmarks of God's presence among us.

Outside the immediate context of worship services, our four leadership commands can also play a part in discerning vocations to Christian ministry. Those who believe themselves called to leadership in the Church should demonstrate their familiarity (in terms of our four Exodus images) with the tent of meeting, the tablets and pillars, the desert, and the burning bush. How accessible is this person to a range of other people and how do they themselves draw strength from their access to the Father? How sensitive and obedient are they to the leading of God through word and Spirit? Do they have the maturity to respond well to the desert—to setbacks, disappointments and the long hard slog, not only the adrenalin-pumping sprint? Do they know themselves called and are they mission-minded—demonstrably willing to take their place among the motley group of disciples in Matthew 28 and to play their small but significant part in the fulfilment of the Great Commission?

In answering such questions, we will quickly recognize that one potential leader may be strong in 'Follow me' leadership but may lack the warmth of the 'Come to me' leader. Another may have the patience of 'Wait for me' leadership but perhaps without the missionary drive of the 'Go for me' leader. If there is potential to develop those weaker areas, they should be no bar to future ministry. But ultimately 'come', 'follow', 'wait' and 'go' belong together, and it is hard to imagine a fruitful Christian leadership that is entirely lacking in any of them, even though these four qualities can be (and are) contained within the most diverse of individuals and personality types.

Church leadership is one thing, but what of those called to lead in education and healthcare, business and politics—those in much the same position as the centurion whom Jesus met, who could 'tell this one, "Go," and he goes; and that one "Come," and he comes' (Matthew 8:9)? How do Jesus' leadership phrases apply to a culture where employees are simply contracted to come and to follow, to wait and to go?

There's something about the words 'professional' and 'amateur' that helps to answer that question. Although we rightly value professionalism in our work life—understood as a proper skill and competence in carrying out our duties—we should equally aspire to the value of amateurism, correctly understood. My limited knowledge of Latin (complete with memories of dusty classrooms and a daily recitation of the verb *'amo, amas, amat'*) reminds me that an amateur is literally someone who loves what they are doing, who brings to it a genuine and heartfelt enthusiasm.[6] And while leaders who rely purely on the law of contract to demand obedience from their workers may produce a reasonably 'professional' (if hardly happy) working environment, it is leaders who are approachable, inspirational, oriented towards the long-term and 'missionary' in their outlook whose employees will combine their professional approach with a healthy and enthusiastic 'amateurism'. The result in terms of motivation, staff morale, output, good industrial relations and a sense of shared vision will prove quite remarkable.

Leadership in the home is not a popular theme today, but it is significant that Paul's word for leadership in Romans 12:8 is repeated in a domestic context in 1 Timothy 3.[7] 'Come to me' will be the primary expression of this parental leadership in the early days, as babies are hugged, cuddled, washed and fed. This close physical proximity imparts love and security to child and parent alike, alongside a colourful range of bodily fluids that decorate the parental shirt and trousers! As the child begins to grow, this approach will increasingly be supplemented (though not replaced) with an emphasis on 'Follow me', as children learn to talk and walk and brush their teeth by listening to their parents, observing their older siblings, then having a go themselves. 'Follow me' also plays a part in later years, where children, whatever their teenage bluster, generally adopt at least some of the values that they see lived out in the parental home and relationship.

A baby generally feeds on demand: the baby cries and is promptly fed. Before long, however, a wise parent will be training the child to wait for meal times, to develop a regular pattern of eating and sleeping, to move from outward demand to inward discipline. 'Wait for me' helps to develop this patience and the resilience required for a secure and healthy adulthood. And finally to 'Go for me' leadership: a recognition of the need to encourage a proper independence in the child, rather than too cosy a dependence on the warmth and security of the parental nest. The various rites of passage along the way—the first day at school, the first night away from home, the final hug as parents leave their child to the joys and temptations of life as a student, the wedding day—all suggest that wise domestic leadership must be constantly seeking to release, not to grasp.

All Christians, of course, both followers and leaders, can face periods of spiritual stagnation, and herein lies a further application of Jesus' leadership commands. In my own church tradition, the first two ('Come' and 'Follow') are often given special prominence in this context. It is assumed, in general, that those who are going through a dry patch must attend either to their devotional 'quiet times' or to the purity and integrity with which they live their lives, for one or the other must have slipped along the way. It's a solution that certainly applies to many, but for others who (like Job) pray daily and live a life that is largely 'blameless and upright' (Job 1:5, 8), such advice can be discouraging, perplexing and condemning in the extreme. The lessons of the desert, the long-term vision of the farmer and the 'Wait for me' example of Jesus are required on these occasions, rather than the easy answers of Job's friends (as repeated, often parrot-fashion, by their legalistic descendants from one generation to the next).

While one tradition may be somewhat colourblind when it comes to the insights of 'Wait for me' leadership, others are equally weak in their appreciation of the life-enhancing nature of the missionary call. Rarely will a man or woman, approaching their pastor or spiritual director from a place of spiritual dryness, be encouraged to respond by getting involved in direct mission activity—perhaps joining an outreach team or helping on an Alpha course—yet for many people this is precisely what they need. Such activity breathes new freshness into their own faith as they seek to communicate it (in word and deed) to others. A pool of water is a beautiful thing—cool, refreshing, renewing—yet there needs to be a proper throughflow both into and out of the pool to guard against the dangers of drought or stagnation. Where there is not enough water coming in, the pastor or spiritual director is right to advocate a 'Come to me' solution and the setting aside of proper time just to be, to receive, to pray. Where there is not enough water flowing out, the 'Go for me' challenge should be both clear and unequivocal.

'Come, follow, wait, go.' It is not the answer to 'The Ultimate Question of Life, the Universe and Everything', like the mysterious number '42' in Douglas Adams' classic book, *The Hitchhiker's Guide to the Galaxy*.[8] But it does provide a useful framework for leaders and followers, parents and counsellors, in our worship and our daily living.

THE LEADERSHIP CALL

In this book we have considered Jesus' leadership as the shepherd, the pioneer and perfecter of our faith, the farmer, and the Lord. We have looked at a dazzling array of 17 leadership qualities discernible in Jesus' own character, and could, I suspect, have come up with 17 (or maybe '17 times 17') more. We have contrasted those qualities with the 'misleadership' of many of Jesus' contemporaries and have drawn some alarmingly close parallels from the misleadership of their day to that of our own. We have placed the 'imitation of Christ' at the heart of our understanding of what true leadership looks like.

We have also been reminded of the fallibility of Jesus' disciples and of the grace and mercy of a loving God whose strength is made perfect in our weakness. We have dwelt on the riches available to us, sometimes in the most unusual places and through the most unusual means—the tent of meeting, the tablets and the pillars, the desert, and the burning bush. We have taken comfort, perhaps, from the fact that leadership in the New Testament is generally plural, that 'we are the body of Christ' and that no one has all the leadership gifts. Yet any thoughtful disciple, looking at the example that Jesus sets before us, will inevitably find themselves asking the question, 'Who, then, can possibly lead?'

One answer to that question is found in the 'Don't follow me; follow Jesus' philosophy with which this book began. It is, as we have seen, a rather feeble response, but at least it removes from our shoulders the challenge of being role models ourselves. Another answer is to lead as best we can, while giving little thought to the effectiveness and fruitfulness of what we are doing—shooting arrows at random, then solemnly painting targets around where they land as we vainly try to convince ourselves and others that that is where we meant to shoot in the first place.

Yet a far better answer is to keep the leadership of Jesus himself as our target—persistently, doggedly to continue aiming in the right direction even though we fall short on numerous occasions. This is the enterprise in which we will experience the amazing grace of God and the empowering presence of his Spirit. This is the adventure through which we will discover our calling and the fulfilment that comes from living out that calling day by day. This is the path of humility, obedience, grace and discipleship. This is the life of the kingdom of God.

✣

NOTES

INTRODUCTION

1 The same observation might well be made of the 'WWJD' brace-lets worn by many a Christian teenager. 'WWJD' ('What Would Jesus Do?') is a question that can only be safely answered by those with a thorough knowledge of 'WDJD' ('What *Did* Jesus Do?').

2 See, for example, Philippians 4:9; 1 Thessalonians 2:6–12; 2 Thessalonians 3:7, 9, and Paul's farewell to the Ephesian elders in Acts 20:17–21.

3 See www.myersbriggs.org.

4 See www.belbin.com.

5 See www.strengthsfinder.com, and Buckingham and Clifton, *Now Discover Your Strengths* (Free Press, 2001).

6 David Pawson, *Leadership Is Male* (Nelson, 1990).

7 Part of the research of Bob Jackson among Church of England parishes: see *Hope for the Church* (CHP, 2002) and *The Road to Growth: Towards a Thriving Church* (CHP, 2005).

8 James Lawrence, *Growing Leaders* (BRF, 2004), esp. chs. 6 and 7.

9 Leighton Ford, *Transforming Leadership* (IVP, 1991).

10 John Adair, *The Leadership of Jesus and Its Legacy Today* (Canterbury Press, 2001).

11 Augustine of Hippo, *Sermons* 371. For a further discussion on the theme of the imitation of God and the imitation of Christ, see M. Griffiths, *The Example of Jesus* (Hodder, 1985), chs. 2 and 3.

CHAPTER 1: ACCESSIBLE LEADERSHIP

1 E.H. Gombrich, *The Story of Art* (Phaidon, 1996), esp. pp. 387, 519.

2 See John Adair, *The Leadership of Jesus*, especially pp. 17–26.

3 Xenophon, *Cyropaedia*, Book 5, section 3:47.

4 Arrianus, *The Campaigns of Alexander*, ch. 16.

5 Compare Josephus, *Jewish Antiquities* 19.8.2: 'Presently his flatterers cried out, one from one place, and another from another (though not for his good) that he was a god; and they added, "Be thou merciful to us; for although we have hitherto reverenced thee only as a man, yet shall we henceforth own thee as superior to mortal nature." Upon this the king neither rebuked them nor rejected their impious flattery. But he shortly afterward looked up and saw an owl sitting on a certain rope over his head, and immediately understood that this bird was the messenger of ill tidings, just as it had once been the messenger of good tidings to him; and fell into the deepest sorrow. A severe pain arose in his belly, striking with a most violent intensity… And when he had been quite worn out by the pain in his belly for five days, he departed this life, being in the fifty-fourth year of his age and in the seventh year of his reign.'

6 The Pharisees became a clearly defined party during the period of the Maccabean revolt (167–165BC).

7 See, for example, 1 Kings 22:17; Jeremiah 10:21; 23:1–4; 31:10; 51:23; Ezekiel 34; Zechariah 13:7.

8 The psalmist may not have been original in his thinking here. In Jacob's blessing of Joseph, he refers to the 'God who has been my shepherd all my life to this day' (Genesis 48:15).

9 Written by none other than Charles Wesley in 1742.

CHAPTER 2: THE CHARACTER OF THE SHEPHERD

1 The phrase 'his heart went out to her' is especially moving in Luke 7:13, following that most awful of human tragedies, the death of a child.

2 Some might question the apparent pettiness of Jesus' cursing of the fig tree in Mark 11:12–14 in this context. It's clear from

Mark's account, however, that the fig tree incident was in reality a serious enacted parable. The fig tree, like the temple, was all leaves and no fruit: it promised much but delivered little. Although figs are not harvested until June, the early green figs should have been available at Passover time.

3 Chaucer, *Canterbury Tales*, Prologue, lines 43–78.

4 Unfortunately I have been unable to track down a reference for this chorus, which may be apocryphal!

5 See, for example, the Magnificat in Luke 1:48, 52–53, the Beatitudes in Matthew 5:1–11, and numerous incidents in the life of Jesus. See also the humility / exaltation theme in 1 Peter 5:6.

6 J.C. Ryle, *Expository Thoughts on the Gospels: Luke*, first published 1879; Evangelical Press edition (1985), p. 171.

7 Docetism (from the Greek word *dokeo*, to 'seem') taught that Jesus' physical body was an illusion, as was the crucifixion. Jesus only seemed to have a physical body, but in reality was incorporeal, a pure spirit, and hence could not die. The Koran was influenced by this line of thinking in its assertion, 'They did not kill him and they did not crucify him, but it was made to seem so to them' (4:157).

CHAPTER 3: JESUS' ACCESS TO THE FATHER

1 J. Jeremias claimed that 'Abba' was based on childish babble and could best be translated 'Daddy' (*New Testament Theology: The Proclamation of Jesus*, SCM Press, 1973). J. Barr's article 'Abba isn't Daddy' disputes this, arguing that Jeremias' Aramaic examples are far too late to support his contention (*Journal of Theological Studies* 39 [1988], pp. 28–47).

2 There are some interesting parallels between this chapter and Matthew 9:35–38. Jesus' compassion for those who crowded around him is followed by an encouragement of the disciples to 'ask the Lord of the harvest... to send out workers into his

harvest field'; immediately the Twelve, then (in Luke) the 70, are sent out to share in the ministry of Jesus. Moses is similarly called to pick out 70 of the elders of Israel in Exodus 24:1.

3 Paul interprets the veil in a somewhat negative light: it covered up the fading glory in the face of Moses, in contrast to the 'ever-increasing glory' of the new covenant (2 Corinthians 3:12–18).

CHAPTER 4: LIVING WITHIN EASY REACH

1 Eugene Peterson, *The Gift: Reflections on Christian Ministry* (Marshall Pickering, 1995), p. 17.

2 Ibid., p. 25.

3 This is an issue to which we will return in Chapter 5.

4 John Stott, *The Cross of Christ* (IVP, 1986), p. 194.

5 Brother Lawrence, *The Practice of the Presence of God* (Paraclete Press, 1984).

6 C.S. Lewis, *The Lion, the Witch and the Wardrobe* (Collins, new edition 2002).

7 Dallas Willard has also written extensively on this theme: see *The Spirit of the Disciplines* (Harper, 1991) and *The Divine Conspiracy* (Fount, 1998), especially chapter 8, 'On being a disciple, or student of Jesus'.

8 Richard Foster, *Streams of Living Water* (Eagle, 2004), p. 15.

9 This imagery is brilliantly developed by Paul in 2 Corinthians 3.

CHAPTER 5: INSPIRATIONAL LEADERSHIP

1 Richard Middleton and Brian Walsh, *Truth Is Stranger than It Used to Be* (SPCK, 1995).

2 Quotation from Shakespeare's *Twelfth Night*, Act 3, Scene 1.

3 This quotation can be found on:
www.spartacus.schoolnet.co.uk/FWWSomme

4 This is also a common theme in the Psalms and the Prophets.
5 It can be implied from time to time: see, for example, Numbers 12:3: 'Now Moses was a very humble man, more humble than anyone else on the face of the earth.' The New Testament certainly contains this strand, most famously in Hebrews 11—12 and 13:7.
6 Pythagoras lived around 530BC, and Plato was writing 150 years later.
7 Xenophon, *Memorabilia* 4:1:1. Socrates lived from 470 to 399BC.
8 Seneca, *Epistle* 11:9–10, quoted in Michael Griffiths, *The Example of Jesus* (Hodder and Stoughton, 1985), p. 17.
9 Gamaliel's identification of Jesus with zealots like Theudas and Judas was, of course, deeply flawed—a point to which we will return in chapter 9.
10 Griffiths, *The Example of Jesus*, p. 24.
11 See, for example, Peter in Mark 9:5, Andrew in John 1:38, followed by Nathaniel in verse 49, and—most dramatically and painfully—Judas Iscariot in Mark 14:45.
12 Os Guinness, *The Call* (Authentic Lifestyle, 2001), p. 73.
13 This is a particularly interesting passage in view of the stormy relationship between Jesus and the temple authorities.

CHAPTER 6: THE CHARACTER OF THE PIONEER AND PERFECTER

1 1 Peter 2:22 is itself a rough quotation from the great servant song of Isaiah 53:9.
2 C.S. Lewis, *A Preface to Paradise Lost* (Oxford Paperbacks, first published by OUP 1942), pp. 100–101.
3 John Maxwell, *Developing the Leaders Around You* (Nelson, 1995) contains excellent further material on this theme.
4 The references are, of course, to Roald Dahl, *Charlie and the Chocolate Factory*, C.S. Lewis, *The Lion, the Witch and the Wardrobe*, and J.R.R. Tolkien, *The Lord of the Rings*.

5 As James Lawrence puts it succinctly, 'People won't follow those they can't trust' (*Growing Leaders*, p. 125).

6 John 14:12, whatever its correct interpretation, shows a remarkable humility in this regard, which could usefully be emulated by many a 'Follow me' leader: 'Very truly I tell you, all who have faith in me will do the works I have been doing, and they will do even greater things than these, because I am going to the Father.'

7 The books of Joshua and Judges act as a salutary warning here. Moses planned his succession very carefully, while Joshua seems to have given no thought to the matter—the result being a long period of chaos and spiritual stagnation.

8 The twin parable of the pearl in the following verse makes much the same point.

9 Compare the joy of the man selling all he has to buy the field with the rich young man who 'went away sad, because he had great wealth' (Matthew 19:22).

CHAPTER 7: JESUS' OBEDIENCE TO THE FATHER

1 Jesus had clearly been meditating on one particular biblical passage in which every 'it is written' is located: Deuteronomy 6—8, with its deep roots in the desert wanderings of the people of Israel as they prepared to enter the promised land.

2 This 'deafness' explains the strange anomaly that Jesus refers to in John 5:39–40: 'You study the Scriptures diligently because you think that in them you possess eternal life. These are the very Scriptures that testify about me, yet you refuse to come to me to have life.'

3 This term is here being used with its more usual negative connotations: compare Chapters 5 and 6, where a case is made for the fundamentalism of Jesus in its very best sense.

4 David L. Edwards and John Stott, *Essentials: a Liberal–Evangelical Dialogue* (Hodder and Stoughton, 1988), p. 106.

CHAPTER 8: WALKING THE WAY OF COSTLY GRACE

1 Philip Yancey, *What's So Amazing about Grace?* (Zondervan, 1997).

2 Dietrich Bonhoeffer, *The Cost of Discipleship* (SCM, 14th impression 1986). The quotations are taken from the first chapter, entitled 'Costly grace'.

3 Ibid., p. 46.

4 John Ortberg, *The Life You've Always Wanted* (Zondervan, 1997), p. 196.

5 Book of Common Prayer Communion service, incorporating the Authorised Version's translation of Matthew 11:28.

6 This is an extraordinary phrase that Paul uses of Apollos and himself in 1 Corinthians 3:9, and of the Corinthian believers in 2 Corinthians 6:1.

CHAPTER 9: LONG-TERM LEADERSHIP

1 Samuel Beckett, *Waiting for Godot* (Grove Press, Inc, 1954).

2 See Acts 5:37 and Josephus, *Antiquities* 18:3. The rebellion took place in AD6.

3 See Tom Wright, *The New Testament and the People of God* (SPCK 1992), pp. 170–181.

4 One of the soldiers involved in Paul's arrest in Jerusalem mistook him for this Egyptian insurgent: see Acts 21:38.

5 See Tom Wright, op cit. pp. 177–181.

6 See, for example, Mark 1:43–45; 8:30; Luke 8:10. There are other possible interpretations of the 'messianic secret' conundrum: see Bart Ehrman, *The New Testament: a Historical Introduction to the Early Christian Writings* (OUP, 3rd edition 2004).

7 See Matthew 10:34; 11:12; Luke 22:36. For a helpful treatment of these verses, and their essentially metaphorical character, see F.F. Bruce, *The Hard Sayings of Jesus* (Hodder, 1983).

CHAPTER 10: THE CHARACTER OF THE FARMER

1 See Justin Martyr's *First Apology*, c.AD150: 'And on the day called Sunday, all who live in cities or in the country gather together to one place…'; also Acts 20:7; 1 Corinthians 16:1–2.

2 It is interesting to note that Martha, who adds, 'But I know that even now God will give you whatever you ask', comes across as more faithful than her sister in this story.

3 Hugh Rayment-Pickard, *The Myths of Time* (DLT, 2004), p. 64.

4 Stephen Covey, *Seven Habits of Highly Effective People* (Simon & Schuster, 2004). The next two habits are also related to the first: 'Begin with the end in mind' and 'Put first things first'.

5 Bob Jackson, *Hope for the Church* (CHP, 2002).

6 Bob Jackson, *The Road to Growth* (CHP, 2005).

7 Jackson, *Hope for the Church*, pp. 64–65.

8 Rayment-Pickard, *The Myths of Time*, p. 65.

9 See also, for example, Hebrews 12:1–13; James 1:2–4;

10 'Epistle to Diognetus' in *Early Christian Writings* (Penguin Classics, 1968), p. 179.

11 As a moving Gospel example of this principle, it is hard to better the story of Simeon in the temple, who was 'waiting for the consolation of Israel, and the Holy Spirit was on him' (Luke 2:25).

12 Rayment-Pickard, *The Myths of Time*, p. 65.

CHAPTER 11: JESUS' TRUST IN THE FATHER

1 Of course every Jew could link his family tree back to Abraham. To be of the royal line of David, though, was far more impressive.

2 Judah treated his daughter-in-law Tamar like a prostitute; the Jericho prostitute Rahab was Boaz's mother; and David committed adultery with Bathsheba before ensuring that her husband was put to death. The genealogy also includes Ruth, who, like Rahab, was a Gentile.

3 See also Jesus' response to his own nuclear family in Matthew 12:46–50, and his intriguing references to his forebear David in Matthew 22:42–45 and to Abraham in John 8:58–59.

4 Dan Brown, *The Da Vinci Code* (Doubleday, 2003).

5 The opening line of a hymn by Arthur Ainger, an ordained Eton school master, written in 1894, inspired by Habakkuk 2:14.

6 The 40 years that Israel spent in the desert are explicitly linked with the 40 days that the spies spent in the promised land in Numbers 14:34.

7 See also the references to long-lasting clothes and sturdy sandals in Deuteronomy 29:5.

8 See Jesus' response to John the Baptist in Matthew 3:13–15.

CHAPTER 12: EMBRACING THE CALL TO PASSIONATE PATIENCE

1 John Stott, *Only One Way: the Message of Galatians* (IVP, 1968), p. 34.

2 Among those healed was the father of the island's governor.

3 F.F. Bruce writes, 'Many guesses have been made about the identity of this "splinter in the flesh". One favourite guess has been epilepsy—a guess which, if substantiated, would put Paul into the company of such men of action as Julius Caesar and Napoleon—but it is no more than a guess' (*Paul: Apostle of the Free Spirit*, Paternoster Press, 1977, p. 135).

4 Peterson, *The Gift*, pp. 47–49.

5 Ibid., p. 49.

6 Ibid., p. 47.

7 C.S. Lewis, *Mere Christianity* (Fontana, 22nd impression 1973), p. 170.

8 John Woolmer, *Encounters* (Monarch Press, 2007), pp. 208–209.

9 For further information, see Tony Lambert, *China's Christian Millions: The Costly Revival* (Monarch, 1999), especially ch. 7.

CHAPTER 13: MULTIPLYING LEADERSHIP

1 *The Letters of Pliny the Younger* (Penguin Classics, 1969), 10:97. The 'flesh of sacrificial victims' is a reference to the animals that were used as sacrifices in the pagan worship of the day.

2 See Wright, *The New Testament and the People of God*, especially Part 4, for a full analysis of this material.

3 David J. Bosch, *Transforming Mission* (Orbis, 1991), p. 48.

4 According to Tertullian, the first race was held to be the Romans and Greeks, and the second race the Jews.

5 Tacitus was equally intemperate, describing Christians as 'vain and insane', and accusing them of a 'hatred of the human race'.

6 Bosch, op cit., p. 17. The final sentence is itself a quotation from H. Rzepkowski, 'The Theology of Mission', *Verbum SVD* Vol. 15 (1974), p. 80.

7 Jesus' cleansing of the temple in Mark 11:15–17 demonstrates the deplorable state of the Court of the Gentiles, the one place where non-Jewish believers could worship—hence his quotation of Isaiah 56:7 and Jeremiah 7:11: 'Is it not written: "My house will be called a house of prayer for all nations"? But you have made it a "den of robbers".

8 There remains a debate about whether the Dead Sea communities were in fact Essenes or a splinter group from this movement: see Wright, op. cit., p. 203.

9 Bosch, op cit., p. 20.

10 Acts 17:4 introduces us to a group of 'God-fearers' in the synagogue in Thessalonica.

11 See Josephus, *Antiquities* xx, Chapter 2. Izatus II ruled Adiabene from AD34 to 58. Much of the success of the early Church's mission was also among Gentile God-fearers: see, for example, Acts 10:2; 13:26, 50; 17:4, 17.

12 The Twelfth Benediction of the 'Amidah'. For further information, see Wright, *The New Testament and the People of God*, esp. pp. 161–66.

13 See Chapter 9.

14 Simeon's prayer therefore portrays Jesus as a fulfilment of the prophecy in Isaiah 42:6.

15 See also Acts 9:15, where Saul is described by the Lord as 'my chosen instrument to proclaim my name to the Gentiles'.

16 Bosch, op. cit., p. 30.

CHAPTER 14: THE CHARACTER OF OUR LORD

1 See, for example, Genesis 1:28; and compare Paul's extra-ordinary phrase, 'We are God's fellow workers' (1 Corinthians 3:9).

2 See especially Luke 1:35, 44, 67; 2:10; 10:17, 21; 24:41, 49, 52; Acts 2:1–4; 10:44–46.

3 We should also note another post-resurrection 'Go' at this point: Jesus commissions Mary Magdalene to 'Go... to my brothers and tell them, "I am ascending to my Father and your Father, to my God and your God"' (John 20:17). In some early Christian texts Mary is described as the 'apostle to the apostles'.

4 Speech to the House of Commons, 13 May 1940.

CHAPTER 15: JESUS' CALLING FROM THE FATHER

1 See John 15:26; 16:7; also, by contrast, 14:26. The question of whether the Spirit was sent by the Father and the Son, or by the Father through the Son—the so-called 'filioque' clause in the Nicene Creed—continues as a point of contention between the Catholic and Eastern Orthodox traditions.

2 This phrase occurs, in a slightly varied form, in Mark 9:37; Luke 10:16; John 13:20.

3 P.T. Forsyth, quoted in *Mission-Shaped Church* (Church House Publishing, 2004), p. 98.

4 Only *THE MESSAGE* and the New Living Translation give 'exodus'.
5 Tom Wright, *Luke for Everyone* (SPCK, 2001), p. 115.

CHAPTER 16: RESPONDING TO THE MISSIONARY CHALLENGE

1 See www.asha-india.org for further information. Asha is Hindi for 'hope'.
2 In 2002, Dr Martin's achievement was officially recognized when the President of India presented her with the Padma Shri, India's second highest civilian award. On our own mission trip, which included painting a clinic in the Zakhira slum, a leading Member of Parliament from one of the Hindu fundamentalist parties spoke warmly of Asha's work before he and I jointly cut the ribbon and declared the centre open—an intriguing exercise in interfaith relations!
3 See also Paul's later descriptions of the experience in Acts 22:3–12; 26:2–18.
4 See, for example, Acts 16:1; 19:22; 20:4; 1 Corinthians 4:17; Philippians 2:19.
5 There is, however, one church in this part of London whose welcoming noticeboard contains the simple and winsome message, 'NO PRIESTESSES'!
6 Bob Jackson's affirmation of the 'gathered community', quoted in Chapter 10, doesn't contradict this point. Building (rather than simply maintaining) the gathered community involves spending plenty of time on and beyond its fringes.
7 Lawrence, *Growing Leaders*, p. 110. The whole of Chapter 5 ('Finding God's purpose') is well worth reading in this regard.

CONCLUSION: LEADERS, FOLLOWERS AND THE CHARACTER OF JESUS

1 Quoted in Josephine Bax, *The Good Wine* (Church House Publishing, 1986), p. 87.
2 The word Paul uses is derived from the verb *proistemi*, which literally means to 'stand before' others.
3 Bosch, *Transforming Mission*, p. 48.
4 In Anglican liturgy this phrase is used by the bishop whenever a church receives a new vicar.
5 More often than not, 'silence' has negative connotations in scripture: see, for example, 1 Samuel 2:9; Job 12:20; Psalm 115:17; Lamentations 2:10. 'Stillness', though, is almost invariably positive: see Nehemiah 8:11; Psalm 37:7 and, most famously, 46:10: 'Be still and know that I am God.'
6 When Mrs T.W. Atkinson remarked in her 1863 *Recollections of the Tartar Steppes and their Inhabitants*, 'I am no amateur of these melons', she used 'amateur' in just this sense.
7 In the TNIV, this word is translated 'manage': 'He must manage his family well' (v. 4).
8 Douglas Adams, *The Hitchhiker's Guide to the Galaxy* (Pan MacMillan, new edition 1979).

brf

Resourcing your spiritual journey

through...

- Bible reading notes
- Books for Advent & Lent
- Books for Bible study and prayer
- Books to resource those working with
  under 11s in school, church and at home

- Quiet days and retreats
- Training for primary teachers
  and children's leaders
- Godly Play
- Barnabas RE Days

For more information, visit the **brf** website at **www.brf.org.uk**